D0761874

The International Criminal Court

Andrew Novak

The International Criminal Court

An Introduction

 Springer

Andrew Novak
Criminology, Law, and Society
George Mason University
Fairfax, VA
USA

ISBN 978-3-319-15831-0   ISBN 978-3-319-15832-7   (eBook)
DOI 10.1007/978-3-319-15832-7

Library of Congress Control Number: 2015933822

Springer Cham Heidelberg New York Dordrecht London

Printed on acid-free paper

Springer International Publishing AG Switzerland is part of Springer Science+Business Media
(www.springer.com)

Preface

Never in history has a single criminal tribunal had potential jurisdiction over the entirety of the world's population, at least in theory. Students of comparative criminal justice will find that the International Criminal Court is a dramatic and unprecedented experiment in international criminal justice, one that differs in marked ways from domestic legal systems or even prior international tribunals. The Court is a negotiated compromise among the nations of the world, and therefore combines characteristics of different legal traditions. Adopting the generally adversarial system of the common law world, for instance, the Court has a comprehensive legal aid scheme and strict due process protections for defendants. At the same time, the Court's criminal procedure includes significant inquisitorial components, characteristic of the civil law world, such as judicial involvement in early pre-trial proceedings and rulings by panels of judges rather than a jury. The Court also incorporates elements drawn from the restorative or transitional justice movement, such as the participation of and reparations for victims of mass atrocity. More than just a hybrid of domestic systems, the International Criminal Court possesses attributes unique to the grave crimes that it prosecutes and its rather unusual jurisdictional limitations.

What Is International Criminal Justice?

At the most basic level, international criminal justice is a thin membrane of law overlain on the domestic and regional criminal justice systems of the world. Though it operates in a separate realm from national systems of criminal law and procedure, it relies on these systems for the apprehension of suspects, the gathering of evidence and witnesses, and the enforcement of verdicts and sentences. Domestic and international criminal justice systems are intertwined in many ways. International criminal justice absorbs characteristics of an emerging consensus among domestic systems, such as skepticism toward the death penalty, and domestic systems in turn look to the international realm in prosecuting international crimes in domestic courts. Nor is international criminal justice a single integrated system, as in the domestic realm: it is a fragmented web of different institutions with distinct and occasionally overlapping jurisdiction, sometimes producing contradictory results. We will see with international criminal sentencing, for instance, different philosophies and practices of punishment at different tribunals—some comparatively harsh and some more lenient. International criminal justice is partial and incomplete, but in the modern world also dynamic and rapidly evolving. Groundbreaking developments since the end of the Cold War—not the least of which has been the creation of an international criminal court—make international criminal justice an essential topic of study.

What Do Domestic Criminal Justice Systems Teach Us?

In theory, international law operates as a set of rules that are universal in nature. Yet the rules themselves are subject to negotiation among states, and therefore reflect power differentials and political bargaining; international criminal law in this sense is not equally representative of all of the world's domestic legal traditions (Findlay et al. 2013: 47). The International Criminal Court and other international justice mechanisms do more than simply pick and choose, buffet-style, the "best" features of the great legal systems of the world. These systems—common law, civil law, and Islamic law, to name the three largest—are more than just the sum of their discrete parts; they all possess an internal logic and a balance, with their own strengths, shortcomings, and compromises. We cannot know yet whether the creation of international criminal courts and tribunals will accelerate the convergence of common law and civil law systems, leading to harmonization and even unification of procedural rights and substantive criminal law across borders (Stewart 2014: 105). International criminal justice may be too different from domestic criminal justice systems and therefore relegated to a separate sphere, limiting any potential "spillover" effect. But the underlying tendency toward convergence among legal systems exists in the international realm just as it does the domestic. Inquisitorial systems increasingly absorb adversarial elements to help reduce the risk of judicial bias and overreach, while adversarial systems increasingly adopt the truth-seeking elements of an inquisitorial system to prevent wrongful convictions. In turn, international criminal justice institutions also produce their own innovations. The International Criminal Court's efforts to involve victims in criminal proceedings and to specifically reach sexual and gender-based mass violence, for instance, are among the most notable.

Why Create an International Criminal Court?

The International Criminal Court is a permanent tribunal that tries the very worst crimes that humanity has ever faced. In describing genocide, Samantha Power has written, "[d]espite broad public consensus that genocide should 'never again' be allowed, and a good deal of triumphalism about the ascent of liberal democratic values, the last decade of the twentieth century was one of the most deadly in the grimmest century on record." Gross violations of human rights, including genocide, war crimes, and crimes against humanity, are not relegated to the distant past. They are still part of our present world. "Genocide occurred *after* the Cold War," she writes, "*after* the growth of human rights groups; *after* the advent of technology that allowed for instant communication; *after* the erection of the Holocaust Museum on the Mall in Washington, D.C." (Power 2002: 503). The creation of an international criminal court would hold perpetrators accountable, unimpeded by political circumstances, while hopefully altering the future behavior of belligerent states and destructive military and civilian officials. In particular, the rationale for the Court includes the following:

- *Deterrence*: Lack of accountability for crimes can encourage perpetrators, fuel resentment, and perpetuate violence. Repeated warnings of prosecution did not stop German and Japanese war leaders from committing serious atrocities during World War II, and the establishment of the Yugoslavia tribunal to prosecute atrocities in Bosnia by Serbian and Croatian forces did not stop subsequent violence in Kosovo, even though prosecutions were well underway. But the existence of a permanent court could change this. The deterrent potential of international prosecutions is debated among criminologists, but the specter of prosecution may provide at least a weak deterrent for higher-level government officials. In addition, the threat of international prosecution may spur countries to begin domestic proceedings against perpetrators. At the very least, world leaders for the first time are aware of the *possibility* of prosecution when they engage in hostilities (Mullins and Rothe 2010: 784–786).
- *Ending a Culture of Impunity*: The absence of prosecutions may help create a "culture of impunity" among perpetrators who believe that they would never be punished for their crimes. The establishment of the International Criminal Court may increase the probability of prosecution because it reduces the significant "startup" costs of creating a new tribunal. Indicted leaders become prisoners of their own states and are subject to tremendous diplomatic and economic pressure. Serbia's transfer of former President Slobodan Milošević to the Yugoslavia tribunal, for instance, was liked to $40 million in foreign aid (McGoldrick 2004: 460; Findlay 2013: 30).
- *Retribution*: Unsurprisingly, one of the major goals of the International Criminal Court is to punish perpetrators for the most serious crimes known. Retribution is the traditional focus of efforts to punish international criminal wrongdoing, giving perpetrators "just deserts" for their crimes. Yet, retribution has limitations as well: determining a truly proportional punishment to a mass crime may be an impossible task and international criminal justice mechanisms only have the ability to punish a tiny fraction of the total number of perpetrators. Nonetheless, retribution remains central to international criminal justice (Moffett 2014: 14).
- *Justice for Victims*: The International Criminal Court is more sensitive to the needs of victims than previous international criminal institutions, authorizing

victim participation in criminal proceedings, a claims process for individual reparations, and access to a trust fund for the benefit of impacted communities. At the center of the efforts to provide justice for victims are restorative justice principles that seek to repair the harm caused by criminal behavior and the damaged relationships between the victim and the offender and within society as a whole.

- *Gender Justice*: One of the more innovative features of the Rome Statute is the extent to which it develops international criminal law for the protection of women and girls. Gender interests are systematically included in the definition of crimes, the rules of evidence and criminal procedure, the criteria for judicial appointments, the duty to appoint advisers with legal expertise on sexual and gender violence, and special assistance to female victims of mass atrocities. The International Criminal Court was the culmination of long-term international legal developments recognizing systemic sexual violence as a war crime or a crime against humanity (Bensouda 2014: 539–540).
- *The Search for Truth*: International criminal trials are not solely meant to punish; they also produce a public narrative of mass crimes. Truth and reconciliation commissions in places like Argentina, Brazil, Chile, South Africa, and Uruguay involved confessions and storytelling, involvement of victims, and conditional amnesty for perpetrators to uncover what happened to the dead and the disappeared. The International Criminal Court captures some of these attributes by allowing victims to make impact statements and otherwise broadly observe and participate in criminal proceedings. An international prosecution is not simply about fact-finding; oftentimes, the facts are well-known by victims and others on the ground. Rather, truth-telling involves acknowledging wrongdoing, especially when performed by government officials in lifting the veil of doubt about widely-known but unspoken truths (Hayner 2002: 25).
- *Norm-building*: Because successful international criminal prosecutions have the weight of the international community behind them, they may help to settle historical controversies and shape how conflicts are remembered by future generations. As Cruvellier (2010: 172) writes with respect to the Rwandan genocide, the International Criminal Tribunal for Rwanda helped to politically silence the supporters of the genocidal regime, improving the prospects for stability in the region. In its search for truth, the tribunal helped to discredit genocide denialism and the erroneous belief among some former regime supporters that the genocide was only part of a civil war or that it was actually contrived by outside powers.
- *Reconciliation*: Despite a long-running academic debate about the trade-offs between peace and justice, international prosecutions may be an integral part of a post-conflict process of reconciliation. Undoubtedly, some combatants may be compelled to continue fighting if they know an international prosecution looms. However, with an emphasis on victim participation and a provision allowing the Court to conduct trials in the countries where the atrocities took place, the International Criminal Court may be part of a broader "peace" agenda of reconciliation after conflict (Clark 2011: 543–544).

As Karstedt (2008: 16) writes, an international criminal prosecution can be something of a double-edged sword. Trials inspire both collective amnesia and collective memory. They "close the books" by defining guilt and punishing a few perpetrators, implying that they are separate from the many bystanders. However, the setting of a criminal trial shapes collective memory for the future, sending strong symbolic messages and functioning as historical archives by collecting and preserving evidence. The formality and impartiality of the criminal proceeding provide morally powerful instruments for assigning criminal liability to individuals and responsibility to states. As Futamura (2008: 145–151) explains, the Tokyo trials after World War II elicit mixed reactions in Japan today, and the authoritative historical record constructed at the trial did not contribute to settling the history of a controversial period in Japan's past, seen as a product of highly politicized justice handed down by American victors. International criminal tribunals have great potential to promote reconciliation and social transformation, but they may also distort perpetrators' sense of responsibility, guilt, and historical perception. If we are to find success in the future, we must learn about the advances—and setbacks—of international criminal justice in the past.

The Organization of This Book

A volume as slim as this one cannot comprehensively cover every aspect of such a complex institution as the International Criminal Court, but it will try to cover the most important and salient points. This book is intended to be a readable and introductory account of the Court for students of comparative and international criminal justice at the undergraduate level as well as the graduate one. Consequently, this book will make reference to comparative criminal justice topics, including those that involve domestic systems. In addition to summarizing the major debates and current academic literature on the workings of the Court, the book also aims to include new and original perspectives, including, for instance, on the Court's treatment of local criminal justice methods and opposition from the African continent, discussed in the final chapter. Each chapter contains a list of keywords that are defined in the text. In addition, each chapter begins with a summary and concludes with discussion questions and further reading that are intended to guide classroom discussion.

The seven chapters that follow explore the origins, workings, and future prospects of the International Criminal Court, from the origins of the idea after the Nuremberg and Tokyo trials through the negotiations of the Rome Statute and early operations of the Court. Chapter 1 describes the essential features of the International Criminal Court, which are unique from any previous international tribunal or domestic court. Chapter 2 traces the origins of the idea for a permanent criminal tribunal from the trials of Nazi and Japanese war leadership to the more modern experiments in international criminal justice in Rwanda and the former Yugoslavia, and their successors in Africa, the Middle East, and Southeast Asia.

Chapter 3 explores the negotiations and framework of the Rome Statute establishing the International Criminal Court and describing the Court's key players. Chapter 4 is on the Court's jurisdiction, including the four core crimes, as well as the methods by which jurisdiction is triggered and a case becomes admissible. Chapter 5 follows the proceedings of the Court from the issuance of indictments through to a conviction, and includes a summary of all current cases pending at the Court. Chapter 6 discusses sentencing, appeals, and punishment at the Court, including a discussion of victim reparations. Finally, Chapter 7 considers current controversies, including the Court's perceived targeting of the African continent and the resulting backlash that this has engendered, the special case of Israel-Palestine relations, and the role of local or traditional criminal justice methods in international prosecutions.

References

Bensouda, F. (2014). Gender justice and the ICC. *International Feminist Journal of Politics, 16,* 538–542.

Clark, J. N. (2011). Peace, justice and the International Criminal Court. *Journal of International Criminal Justice, 9,* 521–545.

Cruvellier, T. (2010). *Court of remorse: Inside the International Criminal Tribunal for Rwanda.* Madison, WI: University of Wisconsin Press.

Findlay, M., Kuo, L. B., & Wei, L. S. (2013). *International and comparative criminal justice: A critical introduction.* New York: Routledge.

Futamura, M. (2008). *War crimes tribunals and transitional justice: The Tokyo trial and the Nuremberg legacy.* New York: Routledge.

Hayner, P. B. (2002). *Unspeakable truths: Facing the challenge of truth commissions.* New York: Routledge.

Karstedt, S. (2008). The Nuremberg tribunal and German society: International justice and local judgment in post-conflict reconstruction. In A. B. David & L. H. M. Timothy (Eds.), *The legacy of Nuremberg: Civilising influence or institutionalised vengeance?* (pp. 13–36). Boston: Martinus Nijhoff Publishers.

McGoldrick, D. (2004). The legal and political significance of a permanent International Criminal Court. In D. McGoldrick, P. Rowe, & E. Donnelly (Eds.), *The permanent International Criminal Court: Legal and policy issues* (pp. 453–478). Portland, OR: Hart Publishing.

Moffett, L. (2014). *Justice for victims before the International Criminal Court.* New York: Routledge.

Mullins, C. W., & Rothe, D. L. (2010). The ability of the International Criminal Court to deter violations of international criminal law: A theoretical assessment. *International Criminal Law Review, 10,* 771–786.

Power, S. (2002). *"A problem from Hell": America and the age of genocide.* New York: Perennial.

Stewart, D. (2014). *International criminal law in a nutshell.* St. Paul, MN: West Academic Publishing.

Acknowledgments

Many people directly and indirectly assisted me with this book. Foremost among them are the innumerable scholars whose work I closely follow on social media; many of their shares and links shaped my thinking and this book. George Mason University's Writing across the Curriculum Program sponsored a faculty writing retreat that was of assistance to me when I was at the final editing stage. Finally, an anonymous reviewer provided helpful advice about the sentencing chapter of this book that ultimately benefited the final project. I would like to dedicate this book to my grandparents, Remi and Dorothy VanSteenkiste. I also thank many friends, near and far, who have become a second family to me.

Contents

About the Author

Andrew Novak is Adjunct Professor of Criminology, Law, and Society at George Mason University, where he teaches Law and Justice around the World. He was also Adjunct Professor of African Law at American University, Washington College of Law. He has written two books, *The Global Decline of the Mandatory Death Penalty: Constitutional Jurisprudence and Legislative Reform in Africa, Asia, and the Caribbean* (Ashgate 2014) and *The Death Penalty in Africa: Foundations and Future Prospects* (Palgrave Macmillan 2014), as well as numerous legal articles on comparative criminal sentencing and punishment. He received his Juris Doctor from Boston University School of Law and a Master of Science in African Politics from the London School of Oriental and African Studies. He is licensed to practice law in New York and the District of Columbia.

Chapter 1
Introduction

Abstract The International Criminal Court is a highly distinctive criminal justice institution, one with the capacity to prosecute the highest level government officials, including heads of state, even in countries that have not accepted the jurisdiction of the Court. The introduction will provide a brief overview of the International Criminal Court, including the development of international criminal law, the operations of the Court in practice, and the Court's position in the power politics of the international system.

Keywords Complementarity · Gravity · International Criminal Court · International Law Commission · Restorative justice · Rome Statute · State party · Security Council · United Nations Charter

1.1 Prosecuting International Crime

The International Criminal Court is an ambitious and relatively new experiment in international criminal justice. At the center of this experiment is the person of the Prosecutor, currently Fatou Bensouda of The Gambia. The Prosecutor is independent of direct political forces, with broad discretion to choose cases. But her power is not unlimited: she needs cooperation of states to carry out investigations, apprehend suspects, and enforce judgments. Every decision she makes must be reviewed by the Court's judges. Not even the United Nations (UN) Security Council, created under the UN Charter, the treaty that established the UN system in 1945, can permanently stop or prevent an investigation or prosecution. Although the International Criminal Court has, in theory, broad jurisdiction to prosecute serious crimes such as genocide and war crimes, in practice the governing statute of the Court, known as the Rome Statute after the location of the diplomatic conference where it was drafted, places some carefully-negotiated limits on the

© Springer International Publishing Switzerland 2015
A. Novak, *The International Criminal Court*, DOI 10.1007/978-3-319-15832-7_1

Court's jurisdiction. In general, the following principles govern prosecutions, which include personal, subject matter, and temporal limitations:

- The Court must have personal jurisdiction over the defendant. This means that the defendant must be either a national of a state that has consented to the Rome Statute or be alleged to have committed crimes within the territory of that state. In cases where the United Nations Security Council refers a non-party to the Prosecutor, the defendant must be either a national of the referred state or be alleged to have committed crimes within the territory of the referred state. Personal jurisdiction is a matter of state consent, except for the comparatively rare situation in which the Security Council refers a case to the Court in the interests of international peace and security.
- Domestic courts must be inactive, unwilling, or unable to investigate and prosecute the alleged crimes. This is the principle of *complementarity*: the Court's jurisdiction is intended to complement, rather than supplant, national legal systems. The Court only fills in the gaps of domestic legal systems. As a result, complementarity significantly reduces the Court's ability to exercise jurisdiction. The types of domestic proceedings that are acceptable to the Court are not yet completely clear. Certainly, a state's investigation and prosecution of a suspected perpetrator would be sufficient for the Court, even if the perpetrator were ultimately not convicted, so long as the proceeding was genuine. The Court would also probably respect the outcome of a truth and reconciliation commission. On the other hand, a blanket amnesty for human rights violators in order to prevent prosecutions, even as part of a peace agreement, would likely be insufficient (Bishop 2013: 392).
- The alleged crimes must be of sufficient gravity and must fall within the Court's subject matter jurisdiction. The Court may prosecute four crimes under the Rome Statute: war crimes, crimes against humanity, genocide, and aggression. The crimes of genocide and war crimes are largely defined by treaties, while the decisions of prior international criminal tribunals have given content to the definition of crimes against humanity. Aggression, defined as the unlawful use of military force, is the most political of the four core crimes, as well as the most likely to implicate high-level military or civilian leaders.
- The crimes must have occurred subsequently to July 1, 2002, the date that the Rome Statute entered into force, or the date on which a state party accepted the Court's jurisdiction (or the date of referral by the Security Council), whichever is later. A new state party is permitted to "backdate" its acceptance of jurisdiction to an earlier date, but not to before July 1, 2002 (Wills 2014: 409).

1.2 Creating a Truly International Tribunal

Criminal law is not universal, and there is no international penal code. Domestic criminal laws, procedures, and punishments vary enormously across the world, reflective of wide cultural, linguistic, religious, and philosophical diversity.

Nonetheless, the nations of the world have set some minimal ground rules that encompass the worst crimes, including torture, slavery, war crimes, and genocide. How should an international tribunal operate? As Boas (2007: 286–287) explains, international criminal tribunals have historically used an adversarial model, as in the common law world, but with significant inquisitorial components drawn from the civil law tradition of continental Europe. International criminal justice is moving beyond this dichotomy, however, developing its own traditions of due process and expeditious proceedings in the unique international environment.

The Nuremberg trials to prosecute Nazi leadership after World War II and the Holocaust helped overcome theoretical objections to an international criminal court on the basis of national sovereignty. However, practical realities to establishing a continuing tribunal proved insurmountable in the postwar period. The Genocide Convention of 1948 makes reference to an international penal tribunal, later reconfirmed in a UN General Assembly resolution that invited the newly-created UN International Law Commission (ILC) to study the possibility of establishing a permanent tribunal. In 1950, the ILC determined that the establishment of a permanent court was desirable and feasible, and over the next several years the ILC and representatives of member states worked to draft an international criminal code. The early ILC reports and the draft code of offenses were never implemented, falling dormant during the Cold War. Rivalries between East and West made consensus impossible. Nonetheless, the same ideas first presented in the decade after the Nuremberg trials reemerged in the 1990s and many became reality (Sadat 2000: 36–37).

In 1944, as World War II still raged, Harvard Professor Sheldon Glueck called for the creation of an international criminal court to prosecute crimes committed between the officials of two states, perhaps by applying a new international penal code. Glueck believed that certain crimes were contrary to the law of civilized nations, and therefore did not necessarily become lawful merely because they were permitted under domestic law. He also dismissed the notion that heads of state or those acting in official capacity or pursuant to superior orders could escape prosecution for war crimes (Glueck 1944: 91–95, 121, 133, 140). In 1950, Romanian jurist Vespasian Pella, one of the architects of the Genocide Convention, advocated the creation of an international criminal court as a follow-up to the Nuremberg and Tokyo tribunals. Pella considered alternatives for the appointment of judges, the nature of proceedings, and the execution of sentences, arguing that "in many cases international criminal law can achieve nothing unless there [is] an international court to apply it." States would be reluctant to prosecute their own, he believed, especially when those in power—those with the greatest culpability—were the ones responsible for the crimes (Pella 1950: 65–68).

Nuremberg was the first international criminal tribunal, but not the last, and the experiment of international criminal justice was further developed and refined after the devastating ethnic cleansing campaigns of the former Yugoslavia and the genocide in Rwanda during the 1990s. Establishing an international criminal tribunal is a sharing process, and the International Criminal Court has built and improved upon the legal doctrines and practical realities of predecessor tribunals.

The Rome Statute is more explicitly protective of a defendant's rights than the Yugoslavia and Rwanda tribunals were, through, for instance, spelling out the fair trial rights of a defendant and granting a wrongly arrested defendant an enforceable right to compensation (Sluiter 2009: 461–462). At the same time, the Rome Statute itself is still living; it includes an amendment process, and states parties routinely meet to address and resolve potential shortcomings.

1.3 The Restorative Justice Movement

Students of criminal justice have seen in the domestic context that crime is not simply a matter of law-breaking; crime also causes injury to a victim. Although the rehabilitation model of criminal justice has dominated the field of criminology over the past 200 years, rehabilitation of an offender cannot erase all harm to a victim, his or her family, and the wider community. In recent years, a new movement has emerged, first at a grassroots level and then taken up by academics, which challenged prevailing assumptions that punishment for an offender is sufficient, or even necessary, to restore justice after a criminal act. The restorative justice movement aims to temper the criminal justice system's overwhelming focus on the offender by instead focusing on the harm caused to the victim. By viewing crime as a conflict between victim and offender, a restorative approach allows both parties to be involved in the justice process, often resulting in constructive dialogue, apology, and an alternative to incarceration. Criminological evidence suggests that taking a restorative approach reduces recidivism rates, but with significant variation based on types of crime and social context (Wenzel et al. 2008: 376–77; Van Ness et al. 2015: 3–4).

The International Criminal Court's structure and practice is influenced by the restorative justice movement, emphasizing reparation of the harm caused by mass atrocity, addressing the material and human consequences of violence, and aiming at appropriate restoration of victims, their families, and their communities. In the Western world, across both common law and civil law jurisdictions, restorative efforts have included victim-offender mediation and family group conferences for juvenile delinquency, to name two common forms. Earlier international criminal tribunals had little to no role for the victims of mass violence; the tribunals were arguably distant, foreign institutions that lacked local legitimacy and perspective. Beyond the divide between adversarial and inquisitorial justice processes, the restorative justice movement aims at a third model, a participatory one, in which victims, perpetrators, and other stakeholders are permitted to talk openly in constructive dialogue (Hoyle 2010: 6–8). Certainly, restorative justice has its limits; one may question, for instance, the validity of its pretentions to be truly universal or inherently a net positive. One may also challenge whether it succeeds in placing the victim at the center of criminal justice instead of the offender and giving voice to women and the marginalized (Cunneen 2010: 104–05, 136). Nonetheless, there is no question that the restorative justice movement has impacted international criminal justice after the bitter conflicts of the past 25 years, and the Rome Statute of the International Criminal Court is no exception.

Mass grave at "killing fields" of Cambodia. *Photo* from Thinkstock.com

The International Criminal Court goes much further than previous tribunals in attempting to place victims at the center of the criminal justice proceeding. Unlike prior international tribunals such as the ones for the former Yugoslavia and Rwanda, the Rome Statute allows victim participation at trial and even provides legal aid to victims to ensure their representation. Perpetrators may be liable to provide victims with restitution, and the Registry Division of the Court administers a trust fund to benefit victims and their communities. Whereas retributive justice involves the state and the offender in a legal process directed towards determination of guilt and punishment, restorative justice involves victims, community members and other stakeholders in a collective enterprise of conflict resolution (Findlay et al. 2013: 108). Like any criminal court, the International Criminal Court's prosecutions are premised on the legal culpability of the accused person. Are the International Criminal Court's attempts to involve victims in this proceeding truly worthwhile, or are they simply window dressing? The Court's involvement of victims is somewhat selective, to be sure, and some observers have advocated participation at every stage of the criminal proceeding, from the decision to begin an investigation to the post-trial process. Restorative justice, though, is not simply about victims; its mission is to restore communities as well, and the trust fund aims to do that through grants and benefits for local services. Whether the International Criminal Court is contributing to a new restorative justice model remains to be seen, but domestic systems may have much to learn from the Court's experiments in victim participation, reparations, and community involvement, features that will be explored in later chapters.

1.4 Questions for Discussion

1. In what ways does the International Criminal Court's jurisdiction reflect a negotiated compromise among the world's different legal traditions?
2. How does the International Criminal Court's structure differ from that of domestic criminal courts?

References

Bishop, A. (2013). Failure of complementarity: The future of the International Criminal Court following the Libyan admissibility challenge. *Minnesota Journal of International Law, 22,* 388–421.

Boas, G. (2007). *The Milošević trial: Lessons for the conduct of complex international criminal proceedings.* New York: Cambridge University Press.

Cunneen, C. (2010). The limitations of restorative justice. In C. Cunneen & C. Hoyle (Eds.), *Debating restorative justice* (pp. 101–188). Portland, OR: Hart Publishing.

Findlay, M., Kuo, L. B., & Wei, L. S. (2013). *International and comparative criminal justice: A critical introduction.* New York: Routledge.

Glueck, S. (1944). *War criminals: Their prosecution and punishment.* New York: Alfred A. Knopf.

Hoyle, C. (2010). The case for restorative justice. In C. Cunneen & C. Hoyle (Eds.), *Debating restorative justice* (pp. 1–100). Portland, OR: Hart Publishing.

Pella, V. V. (1950). Towards an International Criminal Court. *American Journal of International Law, 44,* 37–68.

Sadat, L. N. (2000). The evolution of the ICC: From The Hague to Rome and back again. In S. B. Sewall & C. Kaysen (Eds.), *The United States and the International Criminal Court: National security and international law* (pp. 31–50). Lanham, MD: Rowman & Littlefield.

Sluiter, G. (2009). Human rights protection in the ICC pre-trial phase. In C. Stahn & G. Sluiter (Eds.), *The emerging practice of the International Criminal Court* (pp. 459–476). Boston: Martinus Nijhoff Publishers.

Van Ness, D. W., Daniel, W., & Strong, K. H. (2015). *Restoring justice: An introduction to restorative justice.* Waltham, MA: Anderson Publishing.

Wenzel, M., Tyler, G. O., Norman, T. F., & Michael, J. P. (2008). Retributive and restorative justice. *Law and Human Behavior, 32,* 375–389.

Wills, A. (2014). Old crimes, new states and the temporal jurisdiction of the International Criminal Court. *Journal of International Criminal Justice, 12,* 407–435.

Chapter 2
Origins of International Criminal Justice

Abstract The idea of a permanent tribunal to try serious crimes including genocide and war crimes is not a new idea; it arose even before the Nuremberg and Tokyo trials prosecuted senior government officials for their roles in the atrocities of World War II. Although the idea for a permanent criminal court was shelved during the Cold War, a small group of committed activists pushed the establishment of the Court onto the international agenda during the 1990s. This chapter will explore the other international criminal tribunals that followed the Nuremberg and Tokyo experiments, including the Yugoslavia and Rwanda tribunals and the hybrid tribunals in Cambodia, Sierra Leone, Timor-Leste, and the Balkans.

Keywords Hybrid tribunals · International Criminal Tribunal for the Former Yugoslavia (ICTY) · International Criminal Tribunal for Rwanda (ICTR) · Nuremberg trials · Special Court for Sierra Leone · Tokyo trials

2.1 The Legacy of International Criminal Tribunals

A number of international courts and tribunals have prosecuted international crimes since the creation of the United Nations system in 1945. The first were the International Military Tribunal at Nuremberg, Germany, which was established by treaty in August 1945, and the International Military Tribunal for the Far East in Tokyo, Japan, created by special proclamation of the Supreme Commander of Japan, U.S. General Douglas McArthur, in January 1946. In a later era, the International Criminal Tribunal for the Former Yugoslavia (ICTY) and the International Criminal Tribunal in Rwanda (ICTR) followed these early experiments, established by the UN Security Council in the mid-1990s after enormous human catastrophes that involved deliberative, large scale, and premeditated crimes in the Balkans and Central Africa. Finally, a generation of "hybrid" or "internationalized" tribunals followed those of Yugoslavia and Rwanda, mandated to prosecute both international and domestic crimes. Four of

A. Novak, *The International Criminal Court*, DOI 10.1007/978-3-319-15832-7_2

these were internationalized courts, including the Special Court for Sierra Leone, the Extraordinary Chambers in the Courts of Cambodia, the Special Tribunal for Lebanon, and the Special Panels of Dili, Timor-Leste. In addition, several domestic courts have been empowered to prosecute international law, including the Regulation 64 Panels in Kosovo and the War Crimes Chamber in Bosnia-Herzegovina (Smeulers et al. 2013: 8–9). All of these experiments were temporary and possessed limited temporal, territorial, and subject matter jurisdiction that began after the conclusion of a conflict, except for the ICTY, which was established while the conflict still raged. While these qualities make these tribunals quite different from that of a permanent international court sitting in The Hague, their experience was vital in constructing an institution that resolved some of the more burdensome, lengthy, and expensive aspects of the ICTY and ICTR.

Unlike in domestic common law systems, case law is not binding as a matter of general international law, whether it comes from national or international tribunals. That said, the earliest international criminal tribunals—those in Nuremberg and Tokyo after World War II—have had profound influence on the development of international criminal justice. For instance, the ICTY has made extensive reference to its earlier predecessors. All international tribunals require judges to determine the definitions and scope of crimes and the principles of liability, and judges find prior decisions persuasive even if they are not binding (Cryer 2012: 146–147). The three crimes prosecuted at Nuremberg—war crimes, crimes against humanity, and crimes against peace—have become firmly entrenched in international law, though not until the Rome Conference in 1998 did a majority of states explicitly make clear that crimes against humanity do not need to occur during armed conflict. Another development at Nuremberg that persists to the present era is the use of conspiracy as a basis for international criminal responsibility (Kelly and Timothy 2008: 105–114). Likewise, the doctrine of command responsibility, in which culpability falls most heavily on those at the top of the hierarchy, is an important piece of international criminal law as a result of the Nuremberg precedent. The development of international criminal law over the last fifty years has been a cumulative sharing process, and its principles are not limited to the text of any single treaty or within the walls of a single institution.

2.1.1 The Nuremberg and Tokyo Trials

The Nuremberg and Tokyo trials after World War II were the first attempts to criminalize aggressive war and abuses against civilian populations. With considerable leadership from the American prosecutor, U.S. Supreme Court Justice Robert Jackson, the Nuremberg trial and its sister tribunal in the Far East seemed to represent a triumph of law over power, but they also represented justice as imposed by the victorious Allied powers and did not prosecute the Allies for their own crimes. The United States was the strongest legal, material, and financial supporter of the Nuremberg tribunal, and the American commitment to try senior Nazi leadership occurred under relatively high professional standards. Undoubtedly, the trials were not perfect, but they played an important role in reducing tensions between the victors and the vanquished by substituting a legal process for revenge. By focusing the blame on Nazi officials, the trials decreased the risk that the whole German nation and population would be assigned the lasting burden of collective guilt (Beigbeder 1999: 35–40, 48–49; Bosco 2014: 27–28).

The Nuremberg trials lasted from November 14, 1945, to October 1, 1946. The adjudicators included one judge and one alternate appointed by each of the four major powers, Britain, France, the United States, and the Soviet Union. Each of the four major powers also appointed a prosecutor, and the trials themselves occurred in the American-occupied zone of Germany and benefited from substantial American legal expertise. A total of 24 defendants were indicted, as well as seven criminal organizations. The defendants represented different levels of responsibility in the Nazi regime, and both military and civilian functions. Of the 22 defendants tried (excluding one tried in absentia and one who committed suicide shortly before the trial's commencement), twelve were sentenced to death by hanging, three were sentenced to life imprisonment, and four to prison terms between ten and twenty years. Three defendants were found not guilty and released (Beigbeder 1999: 35–38).

The defendants were charged with four crimes: conspiracy, crimes against peace, war crimes, and crimes against humanity. Framing of the criminal charges at Nuremberg posed an obvious difficulty: what crimes were actually illegal under international law? Certainly, war crimes had been defined by the end of the World War I, but whether the prosecution would be able to show beyond a reasonable doubt that any of the men at Nuremberg had directly ordered or perpetrated any of these crimes was far from certain. Justice Jackson and the American prosecution team opted to pursue conspiracy charges, which caught all of the defendants in the net as they could not claim obedience to higher orders. One problem with this approach was that declaring all those who participate in a conspiracy as equally responsible is unique to Anglo-American law. French, Russian, and German law did not recognize conspiracy as such, and in these jurisdictions defendants could only be tried for their individual crimes. That the Soviet Union had also waged aggressive war by invading Poland in September and Finland in December 1939 complicated Jackson's legal theory further (Overy 2003: 14–19).

American and British prosecutors also wanted to include Nazi anti-Semitism as a charge, but how to frame the indictable offense posed a definitional problem. The term "genocide," coined in 1944, was one possibility, but French and Soviet prosecutors were anxious to include the persecution of their populations as well as the Jews. A new category of offense, "crimes against humanity," was agreed and included the persecution and murder of Jews, Poles, and Roma (gypsies). However, despite the severity of these crimes, the Nuremberg trials left the category of "crimes against humanity" relatively undeveloped, and the judgment of the tribunal did not strictly separate crimes against humanity from war crimes, which included such atrocities as cruel treatment of civilian populations, murder of prisoners of war, enforced population exchanges, and pillage during armed conflict (ibid: 20–21; Beigbeder 1999: 44–48).

The most powerful legal challenge to the prosecutions at Nuremberg was never addressed by the prosecutors at all: that most of the crimes of which the defendants stood accused were not regarded as crimes at the time they were committed. Under the prohibition of ex post facto criminal laws (sometimes rendered by the Latin phrase, *nullum crimen sine lege*, or "no crime without law" in European civil law systems), retroactive justice of this sort was unknown in most legal systems. Jackson explained that the Nazi crimes were severe enough to have been "regarded as criminal since the time of Cain," and indicated that they would have been criminalized if the law had not been so grossly perverted under Nazi rule. The central purpose of the tribunal, however, was not to conform to existing international law, but to establish new rules of international conduct and lay boundaries for future human rights violations (Overy 2003: 22–23).

After Japan's surrender on August 14, 1945, Japan accepted the terms of the Potsdam Declaration, which placed the Japanese government under the control of General Douglas MacArthur, the Supreme Commander for the Allied Powers. On January 19, 1956, MacArthur issued a proclamation establishing an International Military Tribunal for the Far East, with the intention to assign criminality to individuals and reject the charge of collective responsibility for the Japanese people. Unlike Nuremberg, however, the proclamation was not a collaborative process; it was largely an American project. MacArthur appointed eleven judges from among the Allied powers, and the tribunal had one prosecutor, an American. The crimes and procedures were the same as at Nuremberg. However, the Tokyo trials lasted more than twice as long, with 400 witnesses and more than 4000 pieces of documentary evidence, producing a trial transcript of over 45,000 pages. All 25 defendants at the Tokyo trials were convicted, of whom seven were sentenced to death by hanging and the rest given jail sentences from 7 years to life. Dissenting opinions from some of the judges indicated a difference of opinion about guilt and due process, and the Indian judge condemned the entire proceeding as an exercise in victor's justice, weakening the impact of the verdicts. The decision to grant immunity to the Japanese Emperor, seen as a semi-divine figure, was also controversial (Beigbeder 1999: 54–60; Futamura 2008: 60–66). Although the focus of the prosecutor was on crimes against peace, that is, waging aggressive and belligerent war, successful prosecutions also took place for war crimes and crimes against humanity, including the large-scale atrocities in Nanjing, China, and the Philippines. The successful prosecutions were a product of a multinational team of investigators and prosecution staff, and the Tokyo Tribunal created important precedent about the responsibility of senior government officials for these crimes (Totani 2010: 147, 152–155, 161).

The Nuremberg and Tokyo trials sought to prosecute only those with the greatest responsibility. With the exception of an editor of an influential and racist newspaper in Germany, all perpetrators convicted at the tribunals held high positions within the state hierarchy or were high-ranking military leaders (Smeulers et al. 2013: 26). Many lower-ranked perpetrators were convicted not by the Nuremberg or Tokyo tribunals, but rather in subsequent national prosecutions such as the Nazi doctors trial in Germany and the famous cases of Adolf Eichmann in

Israel and Klaus Barbie in France (ibid: 34–35). Subsequent international tribunals have succeeded to varying degrees in cooperating with local or national prosecutions for international crimes.

One benefit of the Nuremberg tribunals—and the later ones in Rwanda and the former Yugoslavia—is that the trial record itself became a historical document. Hannah Arendt, describing the trial of Eichmann in Jerusalem in 1961, referenced the immense archival material of the Nazi regime that Nuremberg prosecutors compiled and distilled. This impartial record has encouraged postwar Germany to confront its past honestly and helped build a powerful German culture of remembering. It has also de-legitimized Holocaust denialism. Indeed, the absence of such a historical record for the Armenian genocide in 1917 has allowed the Turkish government to avoid accountability and deny that the genocide took place. Germany cannot do this today, and the Nuremberg tribunal is part of the reason (Goldstone and Bass 2000: 54–55).

2.1.2 The International Criminal Tribunal for the Former Yugoslavia

Forty-seven years after the Nuremberg tribunal completed its mandate, the UN Security Council unanimously voted to establish the International Criminal Tribunal for the Former Yugoslavia (ICTY). At the time the tribunal was established, the major powers were resisting pressure to intervene militarily in the most destructive European conflict since World War II. The wars in the former Yugoslavia displaced about 3.5 million people in a campaign of ethnic cleansing, carried out through systematic forced expulsions, terror, and massacres, perhaps none as infamous as the destruction of the Bosnian Muslim community by Serbian forces at Srebrenica on July 11, 1995. The ICTY had primacy over national courts and could try genocide, war crimes, and crimes against humanity. The tribunal had eleven judges, elected from around the world, and included three principal organs: the office of the prosecutor, the registry, and the judiciary, consisting of two trial chambers and one appeals chamber (Beigbeder 1999: 146–156).

The ICTY struggled with funding, hostility from Security Council members, staffing, and the arrest of perpetrators, but it enjoyed the support of the Islamic world and profited greatly from the support of the United States and the United Kingdom. The ethnic cleansing campaign in Bosnia-Herzegovina had started in April 1992, but not until February 1993 did the Security Council finally approve the creation of the ad hoc tribunal for Yugoslavia. Only in August 1994 did South African jurist Richard Goldstone take office as the first chief prosecutor, and he still had to assemble a competent international staff. As Goldstone reflected later, "[s]uch delays are not just undignified; they are damaging. It is more difficult for a tribunal to have a deterrent effect if that tribunal is being created in the middle of a conflict. And the formidable operational challenge of finding witnesses and gathering forensic evidence only gets harder as time goes by," not to mention the impact of this failure on victims who sought accountability and redress (Goldstone and Bass 2000: 52–53).

Because Goldstone had little support to conduct prosecutions during an ongoing conflict, he started with low-ranking perpetrators who could be easily apprehended in order to build up evidence and global opinion against higher-ranking perpetrators. As a result, in a sharp departure from the Nuremberg and Tokyo trials, the Yugoslavia tribunal convicted a higher number of low-ranking perpetrators or those with no official role at all. On the other hand, it became the first international criminal tribunal to indict a sitting head of state, President Slobodan Milošević, who was arrested after he lost elections in 2001 (Smeulers et al. 2013: 26–27). The Court's first case against Dusan Tadić was uncomfortable given Tadić's comparatively minor role as a guard at a concentration camp, for which he received 20 years imprisonment. The first judgment was against Drazen Erdemović, a Croat who had been forced under threat of death to take part in the summary execution of hundreds of Muslims in Srebrenica, the first application of a duress defense by the tribunal. Erdemović pleaded guilty and received early release; he later testified against President Milošević (Beigbeder 1999: 156–158). The *Erdemović* decision resulted in a close three-to-two split in the appeals chamber and a powerful dissenting opinion that argued that duress could be a defense to international crimes. During the negotiations over the International Criminal Court, the decision was widely debated and reconsidered, another example of how international criminal law is continually evolving (Weigend 2012: 1220–1224).

The International Criminal Tribunal for the Former Yugoslavia, The Hague, Netherlands. *Photo from Thinkstock.com*

The Milošević trial was emblematic of the delay and expense that plagued the ICTY from the beginning. The prosecutor, then former Swiss Attorney General Carla del Ponte, adopted a strategy that made the trial unmanageably long and only slowly developed Milošević's aggressive military agenda for a Greater Serbia. After upholding on several occasions his right to defend himself, the trial chamber eventually imposed court-assigned defense counsel on Milošević. The compounding of the delays in the Milošević case took its toll: he died during the trial on March 11, 2006, some months away from a verdict (Boas 2007: 1–9). The ICTY ultimately arrested 161 perpetrators, of whom 74 were convicted and sentenced, 18 were acquitted, and 13 were transferred to domestic courts in Bosnia, Serbia, or Croatia. In addition, 36 indictments were later withdrawn or dropped, and 20 cases are still ongoing, most in the appeals chamber. The ICTY aims to complete its work by the end of 2015, though it only recently began trials of high profile cases involving the politician Radovan Karadžić and the military leader Ratko Mladić.

2.1.3 The International Criminal Tribunal for Rwanda

The difficulties that plagued the ICTY were exacerbated at the ICTR because of its relative isolation and opposition from the Government of Rwanda. Between April and July 1994, between 500,000 and one million people were brutally murdered, with the Tutsi people (and moderate Hutu allies) targeted for extermination by Hutu Power militias and leadership in a carefully-planned genocide. The international community was acutely aware of the situation on the ground as it occurred. Not only did Western nations fail to act but they took affirmative steps to encourage Hutu Power by removing UN peacekeeping forces before the worst of the killing began. Only the overthrow of the murderous regime by Tutsi rebel forces in the summer of 1994 stopped the slaughter, but the fleeing Hutu militias fled to neighboring Zaire (today, the Democratic Republic of the Congo) where they destabilized the Rwandan state for years (Melvern 2000: 4–5, 227–228; Chrétien 2003: 330–336). On November 8, 1994, the Security Council voted to create the ICTR, though Rwanda objected because the tribunal would not be permitted to sentence perpetrators to death. The ICTR was based in Arusha, Tanzania, with an appeals chamber shared with the ICTY in The Hague. The Rwanda tribunal had primacy over national courts. The tribunal's statute was based to a large extent on the Yugoslavia tribunal's statute, though specific references to armed conflict and war crimes are omitted in view of the internal nature of the conflict. This was the first time that the category of crimes against humanity was separated from war crimes, and the first time that the laws of war were prosecuted in a purely internal conflict (Beigbeder 1999: 174–175; van den Herik 2005: 281). International criminal law was evolving.

The tribunal faced almost insurmountable obstacles from the start, particularly as it was created over the opposition of Rwanda, where it was viewed by the Tutsi rebel government that overthrew the genocidal regime as poor compensation for the international community's failure to stop the genocide. The first indictments were made in December 1995, and subsequently a Hutu militia leader and a local mayor were transferred to Arusha for trial. Like the ICTY, however, construction of the tribunal was significantly delayed, and the first courtroom was only completed in November 1996. Although the United States provided substantial support, few other countries did. The tribunal also suffered from serious operational deficiencies: poor relations between the prosecutor and the registrar and inexperienced or unqualified staff. Even more serious were errors of strategy and due process by the Office of the Prosecutor, despite the transfer to Arusha of very senior Rwandan leadership, including a former prime minister, former cabinet ministers, a military general, and the propagandist in charge of the "hate radio." Investigations were difficult, defense counsel was isolated, and verdicts zigzagged between rigorous enforcement of due process rights and cavalier treatment of defendants' objections. In short, the tribunal lacked a grand strategy (Beigbeder 1999: 178–182; Cruvellier 2010: passim). The ICTR indicted a total of 95 individuals and convicted 59 perpetrators. Though several trials are ongoing, the ICTR expects to complete its work by the end of 2014. The oddly-named United Nations Mechanism for International Criminal Tribunals (also called the Residual Mechanism) will take over jurisdiction of any outstanding arrest warrants from both the ICTY and ICTR when both tribunals finally close. The Residual Mechanism includes a list of judges to be called upon in the future and provided with a small staff should any suspects still at large be apprehended. The Mechanism will be called upon as needed, and will not be continuing. The Residual Mechanism for the ICTR began operating on July 1, 2012, and the one for ICTY commenced on July 1, 2013. The Residual Mechanism will hear any appeals resulting from the last four cases still ongoing at the ICTY, and the Mechanism retains jurisdiction over three fugitives of the ICTR who are still at large (United Nations Mechanism for International Criminal Tribunals 2014).

Despite doubts about the tribunal's respect for the due process rights of the defendants, one of the major accomplishments of the Rwanda tribunal was that it helped politically silence all supporters of the regime that had overseen the genocide. While one may doubt that the ICTR subsequently deterred atrocities in eastern Congo and elsewhere in Africa, the prosecutions marginalized the Hutu Power militias and the former genocidal regime, which proved vital to political stability in Rwanda and the region. Like the Nuremberg tribunal before it, the ICTR de-legitimized genocide denialism and the belief that the Tutsis and Hutus were simply engaged in a civil war. The ICTR emphatically contributed to constructing the memory of the Rwandan genocide, which today is recognized in popular culture on par with the African slave trade and South African apartheid as among the most serious mass crimes to disfigure the African continent (Cruvellier 2010: 172). Relatedly, the ICTR's decisions extensively helped to develop international jurisprudence on the crimes of genocide and crimes against humanity, producing considerable writings on the elements of the offenses, the intent requirements, and the status of the victims, especially with regard to women and gender-based violence. The ICTR was the first international tribunal to recognize that mass rape may constitute an act of genocide. Although the proceedings of the tribunal had their troubles, the ICTR produced a large and impressive body of jurisprudence (van den Herik 2005: 278–284). Prior to the establishment of the Rwandan and Yugoslav tribunals, the testimonies of victims of sexual violence were very rare in international prosecutions. The recognition of mass sexual violence as an international crime helped challenge the gendered foundations of international criminal law, helping to end impunity for these crimes and providing clear precedent for later tribunals (Koomen 2013: 254–255).

2.1.4 The Hybrid Tribunals

The establishment of the so-called "hybrid" or "mixed" tribunals in Sierra Leone, Cambodia, Lebanon, East Timor, Bosnia, and Kosovo reflected the dissatisfaction of the international community with the Yugoslavia and Rwanda tribunals. The hybrid model was intended to shorten the duration of judicial proceedings while respecting due process, ensure the greater involvement of and impact on local societies, and provide greater financial efficiency (Tortora 2013: 93–94). "Citizens of the affected country should feel some participatory connection to the trials if those trials are to further the oft-declared goals of international criminal justice—promoting reconciliation, developing a culture of accountability, and creating respect for judicial institutions in a post-conflict society" (Raub 2009: 1021). There was precedent for this: a hybrid tribunal was established in the Netherlands in 1999 for the perpetrators of the bombing of Pan Am Flight 103 over Lockerbie, Scotland, on December 21, 1988. As part of an agreement with Libya to retrieve the two suspects involved in the bombing, a criminal trial was held in The Hague before Scottish judges and under Scottish law (Stewart 2014: 158–159). If the experiments in Yugoslavia and Rwanda proved anything, they proved that international criminal tribunals are expensive. Those two tribunals alone staffed more than 2000 employees and had a combined annual budget exceeding $250 million. For this reason, the mixed tribunals for Sierra Leone and Cambodia, for instance, were financed on the basis of voluntary contributions—a method that hardly seems desirable or reliable for a permanent court, but one that avoided the dramatic budget battles of the Rwandan and Yugoslav tribunals (Arsanjani and Reisman 2005: 402).

The Special Court for Sierra Leone was the first of these experiments, envisioning the substantial involvement of judges, prosecutors, and staff from the country where the crimes took place. In addition, the Special Court's personal jurisdiction was limited only to those who bore the greatest responsibility for the crimes. The Special Court was born out of a June 2000 request by the president of Sierra Leone to the United Nations for assistance in prosecuting the leaders of the Revolutionary United Front, a rebel group notorious for using drug-addicted child soldiers to terrorize civilians in order to control the country's diamond resources. Despite an attempted amnesty, the rebels continued fighting and took 500 UN peacekeepers as hostages. In March 2002, the parliament of Sierra Leone ratified the proposal establishing the court, and a year later, the prosecutor issued indictments for 13 individuals, including former President Charles Taylor of Liberia and the leaders of the three main armed factions (Rodman 2013: 64–65; Tortora 2013: 96–97). However, the transfer of Charles Taylor to The Hague to stand trial for security reasons substantially increased the Special Court's operational costs (Ralston and Finnin 2008: 59). The Special Court completed proceedings against 21 individuals, of whom 16 were convicted (including Taylor), two were acquitted, and three died before the conclusion of the trials. One persistent question before the Special Court that profoundly influenced later international criminal law was whether international crimes could be pardoned or amnestied. Although the Lomé Accord included a complete and unconditional amnesty to all combatants for crimes occurring after 1991, international crimes were excluded. The Lomé Accord also initiated the creation of a truth and reconciliation commission before which former combatants could testify in the presence of victims as an alternative to a criminal proceeding, though this commission's jurisdiction overlapped and occasionally conflicted with the Special Court (Tejan-Cole 2003: 158). Here too there were lessons for a future International Criminal Court.

Other "hybrid" tribunals followed. In 2003, the ICTY endorsed the creation of a domestic court to provide assistance in trying perpetrators from the Bosnian war. The State Court of Bosnia and Herzegovina was created as part of the ICTY's "completion strategy" as the ICTY sought to wind down its work; the State Court, a special organ of the Bosnian judiciary, had jurisdiction over war crimes and other violations of international criminal law. Although the State Court faced its own funding difficulties and a shortage of skilled staff, the State Court's proceedings were more expeditious than those of the ICTY (Burke-White 2008: 345–350). In 1997, Cambodia sought the assistance of the UN in establishing a framework for the prosecution of those responsible for the atrocities committed by the former Khmer Rouge regime between 1975 and 1979. In 2004, the Extraordinary Chambers in the Courts of Cambodia were established to prosecute only the most senior leaders, rather than low- or middle-ranking perpetrators, in an effort to control costs (Ralston and Finnin 2008: 66–67). Finally, in May 2007, the Security Council approved creation of the Special Tribunal for Lebanon, established in The Hague, to prosecute the perpetrators responsible for the assassination of former Lebanese Prime Minister Rafik Hariri and 22 others on February 14, 2005. With a limited mandate, the Special Tribunal courted controversy as it was authorized to try suspected perpetrators in absentia with a right to retrial if an accused was later arrested. Despite a lengthy investigation, the perpetrators are still unclear and have not been apprehended, though a handful of trials in absentia began in 2014 (Jenks 2009: 59–62).

Does the hybrid tribunal still have a future in a world with the International Criminal Court? The Court is not likely to address every current or future conflict due to resource constraints and restrictions on its jurisdiction. The hybrid tribunal may also possess some unique advantages compared to purely domestic or purely international courts, such as flexibility, cost efficiency, and the combination of international legitimacy with local sensitivity (Raub 2009: 1053). This may be why, even now, hybrid tribunals are in the works for perpetrators in the civil war between government forces and Séléka rebels in the Central African Republic and for the trial of former President of Chad Hissène Habré in Dakar, Senegal, for crimes committed during his dictatorship in Chad between 1982 and 1990. The Extraordinary African Chambers in the Courts of Senegal opened in February 2013 to prosecute crimes against humanity, war crimes, genocide, and torture by the Habré regime. Habré's trial is expected to begin in early 2015 (Human Rights Watch 2014). In June 2014, the African Union endorsed a United Nations-backed report that recommended a special tribunal for crimes committed by both sides in the conflict in the Central African Republic (Al Jazeera 2014).

2.1.5 Other International Prosecutions

The costs of international criminal justice influenced the debate over possible justice mechanisms in East Timor (now Timor-Leste) and Kosovo. Here, the model was not a "hybrid" tribunal that would prosecute both domestic and international law, but instead a domestic "internationalized" court established as part of the larger UN peace mission in those countries, with funding drawn from the general UN peacekeeping budget. Unlike the "mixed" tribunals, the "internationalized" courts fell within the local legal system rather than apart from it. Compared to their predecessors, the Special Panels for Serious Crimes at the Dili District Court and the Regulation 64 Panels in the Courts of Kosovo proved to be very cheap (Ralston and Finnin 2008: 60; Chiam 2008: 217). The Special Panels in Timor-Leste almost exclusively tried low-ranking perpetrators, primarily Timorese militia members acting on the orders of the Indonesian military, as the Indonesian government refused to extradite more prominent military leaders (Smeulers et al. 2013: 28). The panels were composed of a combination of two international judges and one Timorese judge, with a largely international staff. International law standards applied in relation to genocide, war crimes, torture, and crimes against humanity, while Timorese law applied with respect to murder and rape (Chiam 2008: 213–214). While the crimes that occurred in Kosovo in 1999 still fell under the jurisdiction of the ICTY, a bloated budget and a slow-moving apparatus encouraged efforts to instead provide international judges and prosecutors to domestic courts in Kosovo. Like the Special Panels in Timor-Leste, the Regulation 64 Panels in Kosovo included two international judges and one local judge, with most prosecutions for genocide, war crimes, murder, and rape (Stahn 2001: 174–176).

Not all prosecutions for genocide or crimes against humanity have been accepted by the international community as legitimate. In Ethiopia, the "Red Terror" trials against former officials of the Marxist military junta (the *Derg*) that brutally ruled the country from 1974 to 1991 stretched out over fifteen years and involved marked violations of due process. Twenty-two top regime officials, including former head of state Colonel Mengistu Haile Mariam, were tried in absentia for crimes such as genocide, and 18, including Mengistu, were sentenced to death. While the trials did lead to the creation of a permanent record of the abuses of the *Derg* regime and victims were allowed to testify in court in large numbers, the due process shortcomings of the proceedings and the lack of international support turned the verdict made the verdict appear retributive, not restorative (Tronvoll et al. 2009a: 9–10, b: 136–138, 149–152). The Iraqi High Tribunal, established in October 2005 by Iraq's transitional government, was intended to replace the American-backed Special Tribunal with one supported by the country's own government. Jurisdiction was limited to genocide, crimes against humanity, war crimes, and some political offenses under Iraqi law. The failure of the international community (besides the United States) to provide support or expertise for the tribunal reduced confidence in the Iraqi judges to conduct complicated war crimes trials and failed to shake the perception that the trial was an American project. Death sentences for perpetrators, including former President Saddam Hussein, sparked international opposition (Chiam 2008: 225–226). In 2010, the Government of Bangladesh established an International Crimes Tribunal to prosecute those leaders responsible for serious atrocities during the 1971 civil war between East and West Pakistan that led to Bangladesh's independence. Although the Tribunal has only indicted a small number of people, it has already carried out several of the death sentences, including against leaders who were still active in Bengali politics and were political opponents of the current regime. The tribunal has been condemned by international human rights organizations for its strongly political overtones and for violations of due process (Silva 2013: 63–65). More recently, Uganda's attempts to try a senior leader of the Lord's Resistance Army in a newly-created International Crimes Division of the High Court elicited opposition from human rights activists for the potential use of the death penalty, poor access to defense counsel, and a problematic legal framework (Human Rights Watch 2012: 13–17).

2.2 An Opening

Although Cold War rivalries rendered the debate over a permanent international tribunal dormant in the decades after Nuremberg, international politics eventually returned the issue to the UN agenda. In 1989, Trinidad and Tobago assembled a coalition of Latin American and Caribbean states favoring an international court with jurisdiction over drug trafficking offenses following the drafting of the UN Convention Against Illicit Traffic in Narcotic Drugs in 1988. As a result of the proposal, the General Assembly requested the ILC to draft a preliminary template for a permanent criminal court (Johnson 2003: 93). The ILC provisionally adopted a draft code of crimes in 1991 and created a working group on an International Criminal Court in 1992 (Sadat 2000: 38). The most important immediate precursor to the negotiations over the International Criminal Court was the ILC's draft statute for an international criminal tribunal in 1994. The ILC's draft statute "got the diplomatic ball rolling again," although it created a model quite different from that later established by the Rome Statute. Unlike the Rome Statute, the ILC draft statute required the consent of the state concerned, subject to compulsion by the Security Council. Except for genocide, over which jurisdiction would be automatic, the draft statute created a broader range of subject matter jurisdiction. Because the proposal was founded on state consent, the draft statute proposed encompassing many different crimes with an international criminal dimension, including terrorism and drug trafficking. In the end, the Rome Statute went beyond the ILC draft statute, giving an independent Prosecutor the power to investigate and prosecute even without a state's consent, though with stricter subject matter limitations. Although the World Trade Center attacks on September 11, 2001, for instance, would have fallen within the purview of the ILC's draft statute, the attacks were not to fall within the jurisdiction of the final Rome Statute (Crawford 2003: 110, 140–56).

The ILC's draft statute was modest and did not please everyone. However, except for the jurisdiction of the Court, which was expanded beyond the scope of the ILC draft statute during the negotiations in Rome, most of the other ILC proposals made their way into the final plan for the International Criminal Court. The ILC, for instance, worked from the basic premise that an international criminal tribunal would "complement" rather than replace national prosecutions and that it would only prosecute the most serious violations of international criminal law. The ILC's draft statute established a judicial branch with separate pretrial, trial, and appellate divisions, a registry, a prosecutorial arm, and a court presidency, the basic structure of which was adopted at Rome. With the completion of the ILC's draft statute, the General Assembly established a Preparatory Committee, which met in six sessions throughout 1996 and 1997, charged with preparing a widely acceptable and comprehensive text. This consolidated text served as the starting point for negotiations held at the Diplomatic Conference in Rome, Italy, from June 15 to July 17, 1998 (Sadat 2000: 38–40). This Conference became known as the Rome Conference, and the resulting treaty establishing an International Criminal Court became known as the Rome Statute.

2.3 Discussion Questions

1. What have been some of the persistent problems faced by international criminal tribunals? How could a permanent International Court address some of these concerns?

2. What are some of the relative advantages and disadvantages to establishing an international criminal tribunal in the country where the atrocities occurred? To placing it in The Hague?

2.4 Further Reading

The literature on transitional justice and international criminal law is enormous. For an updated and brief overview of international criminal law, a criminal justice student may be interested in David Stewart's *International Criminal Law in a Nutshell* (West Academic 2014), which is sophisticated enough for law students but simple enough for non-lawyers. Besides the many excellent sources cited in this chapter, those interested in transitional justice may be interested in *Unspeakable Truths: Facing the Challenge of Truth Commissions* by Priscilla B. Hayner (Routledge 2002) and *Between Vengeance and Forgiveness: Facing History After Genocide and Mass Violence* by Martha Minow (Beacon 1999), both of which address the theoretical and practical challenges of accountability after civil conflict. The Nuremberg Tribunal is the subject of many numerous and highly readable books, but students may be particularly interested in *Nuremberg* by Joseph E. Persico (Beacon 1999) for a dramatic account of the trials. One of the most critically-acclaimed books in this field is Roméo Dallaire's *Shake Hands with the Devil: The Failure of Humanity in Rwanda* (Carroll and Graf 2005). Daillaire was the head of the UN mission to Rwanda during the genocide, and he bears witness to many devastating and hopeful events.

References

Arsanjani, M., & Reisman, W. M. (2005). The law-in-action of the International Criminal Court. *American Journal of International Law, 99,* 385–403.

AU backs call for war crimes tribunal in CAR. (2014, June 7). *Al-Jazeera.* Available at: http://www.aljazeera.com/news/africa/2014/06/au-backs-call-war-crimes-tribunal-car-20146781117534173.html.

Beigbeder, Y. (1999). *Judging war criminals: The politics of international justice.* New York: Macmillan Press.

Boas, G. (2007). *The Milošević trial: Lessons for the conduct of complex international criminal proceedings.* New York: Cambridge University Press.

Bosco, D. (2014). *Rough justice: The International Criminal Court in a world of power politics.* New York: Oxford University Press.

Burke-White, W. W. (2008). The domestic influence of international criminal tribunals: The International Criminal Tribunal for the Former Yugoslavia and the creation of the State Court of Bosnia & Herzegovina. *Columbia Journal of Transnational Law, 46,* 279–350.

Chiam, M. (2008). Different models of tribunals. In D. A. Blumenthal & T. L. H. McCormack (Eds.), *The legacy of Nuremberg: Civilising influence or institutionalised vengeance?* (pp. 205–228). Boston: Martinus Nijhoff Publishers.

Chrétien, J.-P. (2003). The Great Lakes of Africa: Two thousand years of history (S. Straus, Trans.) New York: Zone Books.

Crawford, J. (2003). The drafting of the Rome Statute. In P. Sands (Ed.), *From Nuremberg to The Hague: The future of international criminal justice* (pp. 109–156). New York: Cambridge University Press.

Cruvellier, T. (2010). *Court of remorse: Inside the International Criminal Tribunal for Rwanda.* Madison, WI: University of Wisconsin Press.

Cryer, R. (2012). International criminal justice in historical context: The post-Second World War trials and modern international criminal justice. In W. A. S. Gideon Boas & P. S. Michael (Eds.), *International criminal justice: Legitimacy and coherence* (pp. 145–189). Northampton, MA: Edward Elgar.

Futamura, M. (2008). *War crimes tribunals and transitional justice: The Tokyo trial and the Nuremberg legacy.* New York: Routledge.

Goldstone, R. J., & Bass, G. J. (2000). Lessons from the international criminal tribunals. In B. S. Sarah & K. Carl (Eds.), *The United States and the International Criminal Court: National security and international law* (pp. 51–60). Lanham, MD: Rowman & Littlefield.

Human Rights Watch. (2012). Justice for serious crimes before national courts: Uganda's International Crimes Division. Available at: http://www.hrw.org/sites/default/files/reports/uganda0112ForUpload_0.pdf.

Human Rights Watch. (2014, October 22). Senegal: Chad's inaction won't prevent Habré trial. Available at: http://www.hrw.org/news/2014/10/22/senegal-chad-s-inaction-won-t-prevent-habre-trial.

Jenks, C. (2009). Notice otherwise given: Will in absentia trials at the Special Tribunal for Lebanon violate human rights? *Fordham International Law Journal, 33,* 57–100.

Karstedt, S. (2008). The Nuremberg tribunal and German society: International justice and local judgment in post-conflict reconstruction. In A. B. David & L. H. M. Timothy (Eds.), *The legacy of Nuremberg: Civilising influence or institutionalised vengeance?* (pp. 13–36). Boston: Martinus Nijhoff Publishers.

Kelly, M. J., & Timothy, L. H. M. (2008). Contributions of the Nuremberg trial to the subsequent development of international law. In A. B. David & L. H. M. Timothy (Eds.), *The legacy of Nuremberg: Civilising influence or institutionalised vengeance?* (pp. 101–130). Boston: Martinus Nijhoff Publishers.

Koomen, J. (2013). "Without these women, the tribunal cannot do anything": The politics of witness testimony on sexual violence at the international criminal tribunal for Rwanda. *Signs, 38,* 253–277.

Melvern, L. (2000). *A people betrayed: The role of the west in Rwanda's genocide.* New York: Zed Books.

Overy, R. (2003). The Nuremberg trials: International law in the making. In P. Sands (Ed.), *From Nuremberg to The Hague: The future of international criminal justice* (pp. 1–29). New York: Cambridge University Press.

Raub, L. (2009). Positioning hybrid tribunals in international criminal justice. *New York University Journal of International Law and Politics, 41,* 1013–1053.

Rodman, K. A. (2013). Justice is interventionist: The political sources of the judicial reach of the Special Court for Sierra Leone. In L. R. Dawn, M. James, & I. Pordis (Eds.), *The realities of international criminal justice* (pp. 63–92). Boston: Martinus Nijhoff Publishers.

Silva, M. (2013). Bangladesh War Crimes Tribunal. *International Journal of Rights and Security, 3,* 59–80.

Smeulers, A., Barbora, H., & van den Tom, B. (2013). Sixty-five years of international criminal justice: The facts and figures. In L. R. Dawn, M. James, & I. Pordis (Eds.), *The realities of international criminal justice* (pp. 7–42). Boston: Martinus Nijhoff Publishers.

Stahn, C. (2001). The United Nations transitional administrations in Kosovo and East Timor: A first analysis. *Max Planck Yearbook of United Nations Law, 5,* 105–183.

Stewart, D. (2014). *International criminal law in a nutshell.* St. Paul, MN: West Academic Publishing.

Tejan-Cole, A. (2003). The complementary and conflicting relationship between the Special Court for Sierra Leone and the Truth and Reconciliation Commission. *Yale Human Rights and Development Law Journal, 6,* 139–159.

Tortora, G. (2013). The financing of the special tribunals for Sierra Leone, Cambodia, and Lebanon. In L. R. Dawn, M. James, & I. Pordis (Eds.), *The realities of international criminal justice* (pp. 93–124). Boston: Martinus Nijhoff Publishers.

Totani, Y. (2010). The case against the accused. In T. Yuki, M. Tim, & S. Gerry (Eds.), *Beyond victor's justice? The Tokyo war crimes trial revisited* (pp. 147–161). Boston: Martinus Nijhoff Publishers.

Tronvoll, K., Charles, S., & Aneme, G. A. (2009a). The "red terror" trials: The context of transitional justice in Ethiopia. In S. Tronvoll & G. A. Aneme (Eds.), *The Ethiopian red terror trials: Transitional justice challenged* (pp. 1–16). Woodbridge, UK: James Currey.

Tronvoll, K., Charles, S., & Aneme, G. A. (2009b). Concluding the main red terror trial: *Special Prosecutor v. Colonel Mengistu Hailemariam et al.* In S. Tronvoll & G. A. Aneme (Eds.), *The Ethiopian red terror trials: Transitional justice challenged* (pp. 136–152). Woodbridge, UK: James Currey.

United Nations Mechanism for International Criminal Tribunals. (2014, December 10). President Meron addresses the UN Security Council. Available at: http://www.unmict.org/en/news/president-meron-addresses-un-security-council.

van den Herik, L. J. (2005). *The contribution of the Rwanda tribunal to the development of international law.* Boston: Martinus Nijhoff Publishers.

Weigend, T. (2012). Kill or be killed: Another look at *Erdemović. Journal of International Criminal Justice, 10,* 1219–1237.

Chapter 3
The Rome Statute of the International Criminal Court

Abstract This chapter will summarize the framework of the Rome Statute establishing the International Criminal Court, a negotiated compromise among countries of diverse legal traditions. The Court's structure incorporates elements of both adversarial and inquisitorial proceedings, and creates an independent prosecutor with attributes drawn from both common and civil law systems. Other important aspects of the Court's institutional structure include the Judicial Division, divided among Pre-Trial, Trial, and Appeals Chambers, and the Registry, which governs Court administration. The chapter will also explore the status of ratifications, which today includes a majority of the world's countries but less than half of the world's combined population and only one-third of the world's combined military strength.

Keywords Assembly of States Parties · Coalition for an International Criminal Court · Judicial division · Like-Minded group · Non-governmental organizations · Office of the Prosecutor · Registry · Rome Statute · Victims and Witnesses Unit

3.1 The Rome Conference

The Rome Statute of the International Criminal Court was negotiated at a United Nations diplomatic conference in Rome in 1998, "the culmination of a long, somewhat frustrating, and sometimes dormant struggle" that arose as early as the aftermaths of World Wars I and II (Harrington et al. 2006: 3). However, with the difficulties created by the ad hoc tribunals for Rwanda and Yugoslavia, some of the world's more powerful states voiced concerns that the proposed court would be independent of the UN Security Council, which was then becoming a powerful institution in the management of global conflict and peacekeeping. Civil society activists stiffly resisted attempts to subordinate a permanent criminal tribunal to the Security Council. Despite opposition from the five permanent Security Council members (United States, United Kingdom, France, Russia, and China),

© Springer International Publishing Switzerland 2015

A. Novak, *The International Criminal Court*, DOI 10.1007/978-3-319-15832-7_3

the drive for a permanent court accelerated by the mid-1990s. A compromise brokered by Singapore to allow Security Council members to have a *limited* say over the Court's proceedings softened this opposition. The world had changed since the Cold War. In December 1997, for the first time, civil society activists and a coalition of friendly mid-size powers succeeded in driving the issue of landmines up the international agenda without the support of the major powers. The Anti-Personnel Landmine Treaty (also known as the Ottawa Treaty) has been extremely successful even without the United States, Russia, China, or India as members, and the civil society coalition driving the campaign, the International Campaign to Ban Landmines and its American founder Jody Williams, won the 1997 Nobel Peace Prize. The Ottawa Treaty provided a model for justice activists to pursue an international criminal court despite opposition from the world's largest powers (Bosco 2014: 44).

The passage of the Rome Statute involved an alliance between two coalitions that supported the creation of a permanent international criminal tribunal. The first of these was a coalition of governments, dubbed the "Like-Minded Group," led by Germany and such middle powers as Argentina, Canada, Norway, and the Netherlands. At the Rome Conference, the Like-Minded Group successfully corralled many African and Latin American states into supporting a robust statute and ultimately succeeded in establishing a supportive European Union (EU) stance (Glasius 2006: 22–26). Eventually, every EU member except France was in the Like-Minded Group, and all EU member states became signatories. In 2000, despite concerns about its extensive peacekeeping operations overseas, France became the first member of the Security Council to ratify the Rome Statute after passing an amendment to its national constitution (McGoldrick 2004: 392). By contrast, the opponents of the Court—China, India, Israel, Pakistan, Russia, the United States, and most of the Arab world (except for Jordan)—did not form a unified front. One of the most profound aspects of the Rome negotiations was the cross-cutting nature of the debate, one that traversed the Global North-South divide. India, for instance, historically a leader of the developing world, was marginalized at the Conference by African and Latin American nations as a result of its quixotic opposition to the Court (Glasius 2006: 22–26).

The second half of the Rome alliance was a coalition of non-governmental organizations, or NGOs, who represented global civil society through their activism on such topics as human rights, small arms proliferation, gender and women's issues, rule of law advocacy, faith and religion, and post-conflict and transitional justice. Groups such as Amnesty International and the World Federalist Movement joined forces to form the Coalition for an International Criminal Court in New York in 1995, which grew into a network of over 800 organizations, 236 of which were represented at the Rome Conference. Taken together, the Coalition delegation was far larger than any single governmental delegation. The Coalition's members had diverse goals. Feminist organizations were often in tension with a small but vocal group of pro-family organizations led by the Vatican and Arab states, who stridently opposed any language that could be interpreted as facilitating abortion from entering the Statute. A smaller caucus of peace organizations supported nuclear disarmament and the prohibition of specific weaponry, including small arms, landmines, and chemical and biological weapons, an agenda that was resisted by the world's major military powers. The Coalition also included a broad array of lawyer's organizations, law firms, and legal academics, with the familiar tensions between criminal prosecution and defense. Despite these internal divides, the Coalition for an International Criminal Court was unified in support of an independent Prosecutor and a limited role for the Security Council (ibid.: 26–33).

NGOs concerned with gender justice and women's rights played a significant role in the negotiations at the Rome Conference, helping to ensure that female-friendly provisions would be included in the final document. These provisions were of three types. First, women's organizations successfully lobbied for the inclusion of gender-based and sexual violence in the definitions of the crimes prosecuted by the Court. The Rome Statute ultimately included rape, sexual slavery, enforced prostitution, and forced pregnancy or sterilization in the definitions of war crimes and crimes against humanity. Second, the Rome Statute included specific provisions for the physical and psychological protection of victims of sexual violence who either serve as witnesses or otherwise participate in the trial proceedings. These provisions include allowing victims of sexual violence to testify *in camera*, that is, behind closed doors, and present testimony electronically without needing to be in the presence of the perpetrator. Finally, the Rome Statute's "fair representation" requirement ensures selection of women judges. No female judges sat at the Nuremberg or Tokyo tribunals; only one served on the Rwanda tribunal; and only two served on the Yugoslavia tribunal. Additionally, in selecting judges, member states also must consider the necessity of selecting judges with legal knowledge in the areas of sexual and gender violence (Lehr-Lehnardt 2002: 338–345). Even the definition of "gender" was a negotiated compromise, referring to "the two sexes, male and female, within the context of society," apparently to exclude sexual orientation and gender identity as a concession to some Catholic and Islamic countries, a peculiar definition unique to the Rome Statute (Oosterveld 2005: 56, 64–66).

The Rome Statute is substantially longer and more complex than any of its predecessor instruments at other international criminal tribunals. The 128-article text outlines the Court's jurisdiction, structure, and operations. The Conference largely adopted the ILC's proposal but with an expanded role for the Prosecutor, who is able to initiate prosecutions on her own initiative subject to judicial supervision by the Pre-Trial Chamber, known as the Prosecutor's *ex proprio motu* power. In a victory for proponents of an independent court, it is the Court, not the states parties or the Security Council, that decides whether cases are admissible, whether the Court has jurisdiction, and whether a state's internal prosecution is "genuine." The downside is that the Rome Statute is completely dependent on states for assistance with investigations, arrest, procurement of evidence and witnesses, and enforcement of its judgments (Sadat 2000: 40–41). In this way, the Court is both strong and weak: the Prosecutor has extensive leeway to choose cases or situations to investigate and prosecute, but, as will be shown later, the success of a prosecution is highly dependent on state cooperation.

The International Criminal Court in The Hague, Netherlands. *Photo* from Thinkstock.com

3.2 Key Players

In general, the Rome Statute establishes a system with three major divisions: the Office of the Prosecutor, the Judiciary, and the Registry, the latter of which carries out the administrative operations of the Court. In addition to these, other players include the Assembly of States Parties, a body composed of member states to ratify the budget and propose amendments to the Rome Statute; the United Nations, particularly the Security Council; the Government of the Netherlands, where the Court is housed and where defendants are detained pending trial; and non-member states, which affect the Court's investigations and proceedings in various ways.

3.2.1 The Prosecutor

The most important actor at the International Criminal Court is the Prosecutor. Since 2012, this position is held by Fatou Bensouda of The Gambia, a small country in West Africa, and from 2002 to 2012 by Luis Moreno Ocampo of Argentina. Under the Rome Statute, the Prosecutor must be strictly independent. She may not act on instructions from any external source, and cannot be influenced by external sources in determining whether to accept, investigate, and prosecute a case. In addition, the Prosecutor is limited by the requirements of due process: she may not act arbitrarily or discriminatorily, and cannot abuse her power. The Prosecutor must apply the same methods, criteria, and legal thresholds to all groups in determining the level of criminality present in a situation (Guariglia 2009: 212). The role of the Prosecutor at the International Criminal Court is substantially more complex than that of the prosecutors at the ICTR and ICTY, because the ICC Prosecutor must choose the places in the world to focus investigative resources and defer to national courts when they were conducting credible investigations. By contrast, the ICTR and the ICTY were limited to their respective geographic contexts and had primacy over national courts. The political implications of case selection are a far greater obstacle for the ICC than for the predecessor ad hoc tribunals (Bosco 2014: 94). In general, the Prosecutor prioritizes the highest-level offenders, the ones with the greatest culpability and broadest potential for deterrence.

Fatou Bensouda, Prosecutor of the International Criminal Court, in 2008. *By Max Koot Studio* (*Own work*) [*CC-BY-SA-3.0* (http://creativecommons.org/licenses/by-sa/3.0)], via *Wikimedia Commons*

Under the Rome Statute, the Prosecutor is responsible for both the investigation and the prosecution, a broad and central role similar to that of a procurator in a civil law system. As a matter of necessity, the Prosecutor is highly selective in committing resources to investigating and prosecuting particular cases. Similar to her domestic counterparts, she develops a strategy for isolating a handful of individuals considered most responsible. Because the decision to prosecute must be selectively made, a prosecution is an intrinsically political act, with significant political consequences. These are exacerbated when the defendant is a very senior government or military official. Like her counterparts in domestic systems, the ICC Prosecutor is motivated by factors such as the sufficiency of evidence, reliability of witnesses, and seriousness of the offense, but, unlike in domestic systems, she must also be guided by the unique considerations of transitional justice, reconciliation, and peace building in the aftermath of armed conflict and mass atrocity (Ralston and Finnin 2008: 49–50). Unlike the more adversarial prosecutors of the ICTY and ICTR, who played roles akin to that of a common law prosecutor, the ICC Prosecutor is obliged to investigate both inculpatory and exculpatory evidence, and must consider incriminating and exonerating circumstances equally. Exonerating evidence is made available to defense counsel (Mundis 2003: 135).

For the supporters of the International Criminal Court at the Rome Conference, ensuring the independence and impartiality of the prosecutor was one of the greatest victories of the Like-Minded Group and the NGO Coalition. Although the United States, China, and Russia opposed the creation of an independent prosecutor over fears that the position would become politicized or rogue, global civil society advocates worried that a Security Council "veto" would add an overtly political element to the Court's jurisdiction and could provide impunity to human rights abusers. The Singapore compromise allows the Security Council to delay a prosecutorial investigation for 12 months, subject to renewal (Glasius 2006: 52–56). The majority of states participating at the Rome Conference considered the Prosecutor's *proprio motu* power to initiate prosecutions on her own motion to be an indispensable feature. Subordinating case selection to a political actor, such as a group of states or the Security Council, could shield actors from prosecution and thereby discredit the Court. On the other hand, some states feared that an overzealous or politically-motivated Prosecutor could target highly-sensitive political situations; in this debate, the Israeli-Palestinianconflict figured prominently. The risk of a rogue Prosecutor, however, is mitigated by a compromise in which the Pre-Trial Chamber is required to review the Prosecutor's evidence for initiating an investigation on his or her own accord (Fernandez de Gurmendi 2001: 55–56). To this extent, the Prosecutor's powers are circumscribed. As in an inquisitorial criminal proceeding, characteristic of civil law countries, early judicial involvement in the investigation works as a check on an overzealous prosecution.

3.2.2 The Court President

The President is responsible for Court administration under the Rome Statute. The President and First and Second Vice Presidents are elected by and from among the judges on the Court. Philippe Kirsch of Canada was elected the first President of the Court in 2003 for two terms; he had previously presided over the Rome Conference and the subsequent follow-up sessions. In 2009, Song Sang-Hyun of South Korea, a judge on the Court since its inception, replaced Kirsch as Court President. The President is largely responsible for managing the Court's external relations, including cooperation from governments, promoting public awareness of the Court's operations, and overseeing the administrative operations of the Registry and the Judicial Division.

3.2.3 The Judges

The Judicial Division comprises eighteen judges organized into Pre-Trial, Trial, and Appeals Chambers. The Pre-Trial Chamber has authority to issue a warrant for the accused if there are reasonable grounds for the charge. The Pre-Trial

Chamber also holds a preliminary hearing to confirm charges once an accused person appears before the Court. After the Pre-Trial Chamber confirms the charges, each case is assigned to a Trial Chamber of three judges, which is able to convict and pass sentence. After both the Pre-Trial and Trial phases, either the accused or the Prosecutor may appeal a decision or sentence (Falligant 2010: 733–734). Like the Prosecutor, judges are elected by a majority vote of the Assembly of States Parties. Judges are to be representative of the principal legal systems of the world and reflect equitable geographic diversity; they are also to be chosen from two lists, one composed of those with experience in criminal law and another of those experienced in international law. The election process is cumbersome. The voting threshold for judges is high: to be elected, a candidate has to secure the support of two-thirds of all members of the Assembly, with each state casting one vote. All members may nominate judges, and no country could have more than one national on the bench (Bosco 2014: 54–55, 82–83). A judge is elected to a nine year term, and is paid according to whether he or she is full-time or effectively part-time and whether he or she takes up residence in The Hague (Mundis 2003: 143).

The representation of women on the Court is another important aspect of the Court's structure. Article 36 of the Rome Statute requires that there be "fair representation of female and male judges," which is the first time that the statute of any international court established such a requirement. In addition, the appointment of women to legal support and assistant roles may help create a pool of future candidates for judicial or prosecutorial office. The appointment of more female judges may reinforce the Court's focus on systemic gender-based violence, including rape, as a war crime or crime against humanity as authorized by the Rome Statute. Not only does the Rome Statute require fair representation of women on the bench, but provides that judges with legal expertise on violence against women and children ought to be appointed, at Article 36. The ascent of women as international prosecutors and judges has helped reprioritize sexual violence as a serious crime, contrary to the experience of Nuremberg and Tokyo, which had no women judges and where no defendants were prosecuted for rape or sexual assault crimes (Wald 2011: 403–405; Grossman 2011: 649). By way of illustration, the first case heard by the Rwanda tribunal was the prosecution of Jean-Paul Akayesu, who had been charged with genocide and crimes against humanity. Although Akayesu was not originally charged with mass rape, delicate inquiry of two female witnesses by South African Judge Navanethem Pillay, the only woman on the Rwanda tribunal, uncovered testimony of gross sexual violence. Akayesu's indictment was amended, and the case became the first recognizing systemic rape as a crime against humanity. The *Akayesu* case shows that ensuring representation of women on international courts could serve the ends of justice (Booth 2003: 168–172). On the other hand, assigning women to work on gender issues specifically may "ghettoize" women in the international legal profession and could lead to their isolation from the main channels of power. Sexual and gender-based violence is not simply the concern of women, but of judges and lawyers across the profession (Sadat 2011: 660).

3.2.4 The Registrar

In addition to the Court's "legal" side, the institution also possesses a significant administrative side. The Registry is responsible for the non-judicial aspects of Court administration: ensuring the security of victims and witnesses, admitting defense counsel to practice before the Court, conducting public information and outreach, and providing services to victims who participate in Court proceedings. Since 2003, the Court has had three Registrars serving single five-year terms: French judge Bruno Cathala (2003–2008), Italian prosecutor Silvana Arbia (2008–2013), and the Dutch jurist Herman von Hebel (since 2013), previously the deputy registrar of the Special Court for Sierra Leone. Like the President of the Court, the Registrar and Deputy Registrar are elected by the Court judges. The Registrar of the Court, along with the Prosecutor and the President, serves as one of the three major power centers of the Court, but the role is considerably less diplomatic and more technical (Bosco 2014: 93). According to Article 43 of the Rome Statute, the Registrar is also responsible for the Victims and Witnesses Unit, which provides protective measures and security arrangements as well as counseling, with specific expertise in trauma related to crimes of sexual violence.

The Registry is also responsible for safekeeping evidence. The Court requires fully functioning and reliable technological infrastructure, as it is based on the model of an "electronic court," enabling it to handle tens of thousands of documents and exhibits that will be submitted in electronic form. To the extent possible, evidence will be presented in electronic form, including testimony by witnesses through video link and prior recording (Kaul 2005: 371–372). In the early years of the ICC, the majority of its documentary evidence was collected in hard copy, just as at the Yugoslavia and Rwanda tribunals, at which point it was scanned and assigned a sequential number. The digital copy was disclosed to the defense and presented to the court electronically. Currently, two of the Court's three courtrooms are fully electronic. Although the ICC has come to embrace new technological tools such as videoconferencing, broadcast technology, electronically-stored information, internal private messaging among the parties and support staff, and electronic search functions, the Court faces unique challenges due to the large scale of its cases. One of these is the existence of "big data"—that is, data sets that are so large that they are difficult to process by traditional means. Although the Nuremberg tribunal was able to organize and present evidence very quickly using only traditional record-keeping, wrapping up trials within one year's time, the ICC faces new and pressing electronic challenges that may be prohibitively costly, such as forensic recovery of destroyed electronic data (Dillon and Beresford 2014: 1–7).

3.2.5 The Assembly of States Parties

All countries that ratify the Rome Statute secure a seat in the Assembly of States Parties, which provides broad oversight of the Court's budget and operations. The Statute does not allow the Assembly to direct investigations or curb the power of the Prosecutor or the judges. All states parties have an equal vote (Bosco 2014: 54). On matters of substance, decisions of the Assembly must be approved by a two-thirds majority, while on procedural matters a simple majority will suffice. The Assembly may also approve amendments to the Rome Statute by a two-thirds majority of states parties, though consensus is preferred. A substantive amendment also requires ratification by seven-eighths of states parties to enter into force, and a state that has refused to ratify an amendment to the definitions of one of the four core crimes opts out of the Court's jurisdiction for that crime once that amendment enters into force. At its first meeting in 2002, the Assembly passed a cooperation agreement with the United Nations, an agreement protecting the privileges and immunities of Court personnel, financial regulations for the Court, and rules for the nomination and election of the Prosecutor and judges. The agreement on privileges and immunities ensures that Court personnel are not arrested, searched, or detained while engaging in an investigation, and that their documents and personal effects are not seized (Mundis 2003: 132–139). The Assembly of States Parties elects its own president, the first of whom was Prince Zeid of Jordan (one of the few Arab states parties), who later chaired the working group on the crime of aggression and was elected UN High Commissioner for Human Rights in August 2014.

The primary job of the Assembly is to ensure the Court's budget. The absence of the United States from the International Criminal Court regime raises significant concerns about the budget's future health. The United States was the largest contributor to the Yugoslav and Rwanda tribunals, which were large and expensive institutions. The Yugoslav tribunal, for instance, had a staff of 1200 and a budget of $271 million at its peak, and the Rwanda tribunal was only slightly smaller (over 870 staff and a $177 million budget). Current American law prohibits providing financial support to the Court since the United States has withdrawn from the Rome Statute (Wippman 2006: 105). The Assembly has had greater luck from the Court's other members. Japan and Germany have historically been the largest funders, each providing about twenty percent of the Court's budget. Linking judicial appointments to budget contributions may become a source of subtle pressure on judicial independence, but it is a concession to practical reality. The largest contributors to the Court include Japan, Germany, France, United Kingdom, Italy, Canada, Spain, Brazil, Netherlands, and South Korea, most of which were prominent members of the Like-Minded Group at the Rome Conference (Bosco 2014: 82–83, 135).

3.2.6 The United States of America

Despite playing an active role at the Rome Conference, the United States, though not the only country to oppose creation of the International Criminal Court, became its most vocal opponent in the early years. While other major powers such as China, India, and Russia also expressed concerns with the constraint on sovereignty that allowed an international body to prosecute their own nationals, these countries were content with simply failing to ratify the Rome Statute. By contrast, the United States actively opposed the Court's jurisdiction, especially the independent Prosecutor (Glasius 2006: 17). The opposition of the United States even extended to undermining the support of other nations and hindering the Court's operations. Recognizing the emerging domestic opposition to the Court, outgoing U.S. President Bill Clinton nonetheless signed the Rome Statute in 2000, accompanied by a signing statement that recognized the Court's "significant flaws" such as potential jurisdiction over non-members (Fairlie 2011: 533).

It fell to the George W. Bush administration to formulate the early American strategy toward the Court. This strategy included four prongs, and was prominently advanced by John Bolton, then a deputy undersecretary of state and later U.S. ambassador to the United Nations (ibid.: 537). First, in May 2002, the United States Congress passed the American Servicemembers Protection Act, which was designed to shield members of the U.S. armed forces and official personnel from the jurisdiction of the International Criminal Court. Most controversially, the Act authorized the U.S. President "to use all means necessary and appropriate" to bring release of any American held by the Court. Consequently, NGOs dubbed the law the "Hague Invasion Act." Congressional opposition decreased in succeeding years, but prominent world issues such as a flare-up of the Israeli-Palestinian conflict may trigger additional activity on Capitol Hill. Second, also in May 2002, the George W. Bush administration wrote to the United Nations to "unsign" the Rome Statute, the legality of which is contested. Third, in June 2002, the United States successfully pressured the Security Council to defer any investigation or prosecution of UN peacekeeping troops whose state of nationality was not a party to the Court, an additional protection for American nationals serving on UN missions. However, after the Abu Ghraib scandal in 2004 in which American troops were found complicit in the torturous confessions of Iraqi prisoners, the Security Council failed to renew the peacekeeper immunity provisions (Glasius 2006: 18–21).

The fourth prong of the early American policy toward the Court was to pressure the Court's allies not to transfer American nationals to The Hague. Beginning in August 2002, the United States negotiated bilateral non-surrender agreements with other states parties. The first country to sign such an agreement with the United States was Romania, sparking a backlash from the European Union. In total, at least fifty-three states parties signed such agreements, most of them in the developing world, and many on threat of suspension of American military aid (Glasius 2006: 18–21). Article 98 of the Rome Statute provides that the Court may not request surrender of a suspect or fugitive if that request would be inconsistent with obligations under other international agreements. For instance, if State A and State B agree with each other not to surrender each other's nationals to the Court without prior consent, neither state is obliged to honor an ICC request to turn over nationals of the other state. In the early years of the Court, more than 100 such "Article 98" agreements were concluded, typically providing that the national of one party present in the territory of the other party cannot be surrendered to the Court. Despite the early support of the United States for such agreements, the use of Article 98 agreements gradually ended and no new agreements have been concluded in recent years (Stewart 2014: 155–56).

Opposition from the United States eventually waned. The reelection of George W. Bush in 2004 led to an administration that was significantly less "neo-conservative" than his first administration, and Secretary of State Condoleezza Rice was pivotal in convincing the Bush administration not to veto the Security Council's referral of Sudan for the Darfur genocide. The United States ultimately abstained, along with China, Brazil, and Algeria, and the referral went forward. By the end of the Bush administration, American government officials had met with the Prosecutor and other Court personnel on several occasions. The administration of President Barack Obama has been even friendlier to the Court, though still formally opposed to ratification. Obama created a new interagency working group on the ICC, and the Prosecutor, Court President, other officials attended meetings with American leaders. The U.S. Government began cooperating with investigations, the transfer of evidence and witnesses, and apprehension of indictees and suspects. On February 26, 2011, the United States voted *for* UN Security Council Resolution 1970 referring to the International Criminal Court the repressive violence against protestors in Libya by the regime of Muammar Gaddafi (Bosco 2014: 111–112, 153–155). Even though the United States is unlikely to ratify the Rome Statute, United States foreign policy has made a significant shift. Sabharwal (2012: 316) is optimistic, noting that the Obama administration has begun sending observers to the meetings of the Assembly of States Parties and no longer ties economic assistance to the signing of bilateral Article 98 agreements. It may also be that the United States recognizes the caution with which the two ICC Prosecutors have exercised their powers, reducing fears of a rogue or overzealous prosecutor willing to target politically controversial cases (Fairlie 2011: 546–547). The United States also played an active role at the Kampala Review Conference in 2010, where the states parties of the Court negotiated the definition of the crime of aggression that broadly reflected the American position. However, this increasing engagement should not be confused with real support or serious consideration of membership (Aronsson 2011: 8–9; Fairlie 2011: 557–558).

3.2.7 Other Non-members

One hundred and twenty states voted in favor of the Rome Statute, including three members of the Security Council, United Kingdom, France, and Russia. China and the United States were among seven states to vote against (the others are thought to be Libya, Iraq, Israel, Qatar, and Yemen, though the vote was not recorded), and 21 states abstained (McGoldrick 2004: 390). One shortcoming in the current scope of the Court's current geographic jurisdiction is the absence of many states that are currently experiencing ongoing internal conflict, though important exceptions include such states parties as Afghanistan, Central African Republic, Colombia, and Democratic Republic of the Congo. Chapman and Chaudoin (2013:

409) found that countries with past histories of internal conflict were much less likely to join the court, as were countries with weak domestic political and judicial institutions. In addition, though nearly two-thirds (63 %) of the countries of the world are states parties to the International Criminal Court, the world's non-members make up 67 % of the global population and a full 73 % of global armed forces personnel (Bosco 2014: 5-7).

China and Russia have remained firmly outside the International Criminal Court regime. At the Rome Conference, China objected to the Court's broad jurisdiction and threats to Chinese sovereignty. Unlike the United States, however, China and Russia did not actively campaign against the Court, and both routinely send observers to public briefings and to the Assembly of States Parties. Their diplomats in The Hague are in contact with the Prosecutor's office. Although China voted against the Rome Statute, the country's negotiators played an active role in drafting it. China's political leaders believe that the Rome Statute does not sufficiently protect state sovereignty since its jurisdiction is not completely voluntary and since the Court may prosecute internal, as well as international, armed conflict. While Chinese leaders have offered cautiously supportive statements of the Court in recent years, the country has also actively defended the United States and other opponents of the Court (Dukalskis and Johansen 2013: 586–589). Nonetheless, when the Security Council referred the Sudanese case involving the Darfur genocide to the Prosecutor, neither China nor Russia threatened to veto the referral even though both took a protective stance toward Sudan (Bosco 2014: 133).

India is a more complex case. The world's largest democracy abstained at the Rome Conference and has chosen to remain outside the Court. Indian officials express misgivings about the Court's design, and academic and media commentary have been hostile. Senior officials privately concede that membership is unlikely, and the potential for hostilities with Pakistan and militants in Kashmir make accepting the Court's jurisdiction difficult (Bosco 2014: 133–34). India has been consistently critical of the makeup of the Security Council—the country does not hold a permanent veto even though it will be the world's most populous country by 2025—and consequently it opposes the Security Council referral mechanism and deferral power (McGoldrick 2004: 440). India's position on the International Criminal Court can be characterized as ambivalent, and the Indian government has publicly attempted to find "common ground" between the United States and Court supporters while cooperating with the American campaign to undermine the Court. The country objects to the limitations on its national sovereignty and perceives the Court to be subject to subtle political manipulation. India's perplexing disinterest in the Court is a serious setback for supporters (Banerjee 2011: 459, 472–476). Unlike India, Bangladesh ratified the Rome Statute in 2010 as part of a package of reforms that laid the groundwork for criminal prosecutions for perpetrators in the 1971 War of Independence. Bangladesh, a small but populous country with significant economic potential, looked to the Rome Statute as a model for launching its own domestic prosecutions (Dukalskis and Johansen 2013: 584–586).

Japan was much more promising from the outset. Although Japan initially echoed many American concerns of the Rome Statute, the country opted to observe the Court in action before joining. Officials from the Court and from European delegations made courting Japan a top priority, seeing it as a "softer" opponent than India, Russia, or China. Japan was hesitant to embrace the Court while the United States, its closest military ally, remained hostile, but after American opposition softened during George W. Bush's second term, Japan formally ratified the Rome Statute and displaced Germany as the Court's largest donor. Securing Japanese ratification after a multiyear effort was one of the greatest successes of the Court's advocates (Bosco 2014: 134–35). South Korea, which had been colonized by Japan and engages Japan as an economic competitor, was an early Court supporter, ratifying in 2002. Today, Japan promotes the Court's interests overseas, including recent lobbying of the Philippines to ratify the Rome Statute (Dukalskis and Johansen 2013: 581–584).

Turkey is another significant non-party to the Court because it remains a candidate country for entry into the European Union, and its refusal to sign the Rome Statute conflicts with the EU's common foreign policy toward the Court. The European Commission has indicated that Turkey's refusal to join the Court could hinder Turkey's accession to the EU (McGoldrick 2004: 394). Like Turkey, Israel is a non-party, perhaps a historical irony given the central role that the Holocaust played in the development of international criminal justice. Israel was one of the seven states to vote against the Court. Israel's primary concern was the possibility of prosecution of Jewish settlers in settlements based in the occupied territories of Palestine, as settlements in occupied territory may constitute a war crime under some circumstances and international law has not resolved the legality of Israeli occupation of Palestine. Although Israel initially signed the Rome Statute, it followed the United States in "unsigning" the Statute in August 2002, indicating that it will not join the Court until the Middle East crisis is resolved, especially with recent military incursions in the Gaza Strip (ibid.: 439).

3.2.8 The United Nations

At the Rome Conference, the Netherlands was the only state to offer to host the Court. Consequently the Court today is based in The Hague, though it may sit elsewhere if it considers this desirable. The Hague is additionally the headquarters of other international judicial tribunals such as the International Court of Justice, the ICTY, the ICTR Appeals Chamber, the Permanent Court of International Arbitration, the Iran-United States Claims Tribunal, and the Special Tribunal for Lebanon. Of these, the International Court of Justice in the Peace Palace is the most visible, serving in essence as the judicial branch of the United Nations, where it resolves disputes between UN member states—most often disputes over land and maritime boundaries—and issues advisory opinions brought by international legal actors. Unlike the International Court of Justice, the International Criminal Court is technically independent of the United Nations, though the United Nations played a central role in (and funded the process of) the Court's creation. The Rome Statute obligates the United Nations to provide funds for expenses incurred by Security Council referrals.

A Relationship Agreement between the Court and the United Nations was concluded in 2004, ensuring cooperation and sharing of information between the two agencies. This cooperation includes facilitating the testimony of UN officials and providing documents to the Court. Unlike the ICTY and ICTR, the ICC does not need to seek permission from the UN to secure UN documents and testimony in each instance, which will likely expedite investigations and proceedings. One concern of close cooperation between the UN and the Court, however, is that it may turn the entire UN system into a "long arm investigator" and discourage a state's cooperation with the UN. Such cooperation is also likely to disproportionately benefit the Prosecutor over the defense team at trial, especially if UN documents are found to be confidential or privileged and cannot be publicly released (Mundis 2003: 135–137). However, the importance of a strong UN presence in several countries where the Court's investigations are ongoing, such as Central African Republic and the Democratic Republic of the Congo, will greatly facilitate the ability of the Court to gather evidence.

3.2.9 The Government of the Netherlands

A separate Headquarters Agreement between the Court and the Government of the Netherlands was ratified by the Assembly of States Parties in 2006. The Court's permanent premises is set to open in late 2015, designed by the Danish architect firm Schmidt Hammer Lassen, the winner of an architectural design competition organized by the Dutch government. Until then, the Court is housed in a former KPN Telecom building, though the facility lacks adequate space and is a considerable distance from the detention center (Schabas 2007: 342–345). Before and during trial, defendants are held across town in a Dutch detention center in a subdistrict of The Hague known as Scheveningen, where the ICC leases twelve cells. The Registrar manages the Court's relationship with the detention center. Besides hosting the Court's operations and housing prisoners awaiting trial, the Netherlands has also made a substantial commitment to the transport and lodging of witnesses, victims, legal professionals, and staff who participate in the Court's proceedings.

Haaglanden Prison in Scheveningen, The Hague, where defendants are held during proceedings before the International Criminal Court and the International Criminal Tribunal for the Former Yugoslavia. *By Jvhertum* (*Own work*) (*Public domain*), **via** *Wikimedia Commons*

One question to watch in coming years is whether trial proceedings before the International Criminal Court are subject to the legal and constitutional requirements of the European Convention on Human Rights simply due to the presence of the International Criminal Court on Dutch (and therefore European) soil. In 2012, a Dutch court ruled that the Government of the Netherlands cannot shirk its responsibilities under the European Convention, including the responsibility to grant asylum to a person fleeing persecution, simply by transferring those responsibilities to an international organization. The case arose when four witnesses from the Democratic Republic of the Congo testified at the International Criminal Court against Congolese President Joseph Kabila. After their testimony, the witnesses sought asylum in the Netherlands because they feared reprisal from the Congolese government. The result was a conflict of law that was not contemplated by the Headquarters Agreement, as the Government of the Netherlands and the International Criminal Court each believed the other had jurisdiction over the witnesses. The European Court of Human Rights ultimately disagreed with the Dutch Court that the Netherlands had a responsibility to the witnesses under the European Convention, finding that the Convention did not apply to the International Criminal Court simply because of the presence of the Court in the

Netherlands (Irving 2014). After two years in detention, the Netherlands eventually denied the witnesses asylum and returned them to the Democratic Republic of the Congo because they might have been complicit in serious crimes. Human rights observers criticized the Court for failing to protect the witnesses when it determined that they would not be prosecuted for those crimes (Bueno 2014).

3.3 Discussion Questions

1. How does the Rome Statute of the International Criminal Court improve on the experiences of predecessor international criminal tribunals such as the ICTR and ICTY? What new obstacles has it encountered?
2. Do you think that non-member states have good reasons for refusing to engage with the Court? What reasons do you think are the most justifiable?

3.4 Further Reading

The seminal work on the Rome Statute and the International Criminal Court, including the Court's origins and structure, is the monumental book by William Schabas, *An Introduction to the International Criminal Court* (Cambridge University Press 2011), now in its fourth edition. As an introductory text, the book is lengthy and detailed, but exhaustive. For a comprehensive analysis of United States foreign policy toward the International Criminal Court, investigative journalist Erna Paris's book *The Sun Climbs Slow: The International Criminal Court and the Struggle for Justice* (Seven Stories Press 2009), though several years old, is highly readable. The most recent addition to the literature on the origins and operations of the International Criminal Court is David Bosco's *Rough Justice: The International Criminal Court in a World of Power Politics* (Oxford University Press 2014). Bosco's book traces the origins of the Rome Statute and the early operations of the Court through each recent case, ultimately grasping the Court's central contradiction between its obsessively nonpolitical mandate and its highly politicized operations. The United States features prominently in Bosco's book, as do the other major powers. A new book from Routledge also compares different foreign and domestic policies toward the International Criminal Court: Yvonne Dutton, *Rules, Politics, and the International Criminal Court: Committing to the Court* (Routledge 2013).

References

Aronsson, L. (2011). Europe and America: Still worlds apart on the International Criminal Court. *European Political Science, 10*, 3–10.
Banerjee, R. (2011). Rome Statute and India: An analysis of India's attitude towards the International Criminal Court. *Journal of East Asian and International Law, 4*, 457–476.

Booth, C. (2003). Prospects and issues for the International Criminal Court: Lessons from Yugoslavia and Rwanda. In Philippe Sands (Ed.), *From Nuremberg to the Hague: The future of international criminal justice* (pp. 157–192). New York: Cambridge University Press.

Bosco, D. (2014). *Rough justice: The International Criminal Court in a world of power politics.* New York: Oxford University Press.

Bueno, O. (2014, July 8). Criminals or victims? The complexities of addressing the requests of ICC witnesses for asylum. *International Justice Monitor.* http://www.ijmonitor.org/2014/07/criminals-or-victims-the-complexities-of-addressing-the-requests-of-icc-witnesses-for-asylum.

Chapman, T. L., & Chaudoin, S. (2013). Ratification patterns and the International Criminal Court. *International Studies Quarterly, 57,* 400–409.

Dillon, M., & Beresford, D. (2014). Electronic courts and the challenges in managing evidence: A view from inside the International Criminal Court. *International Journal for Court Administration, 6,* 1. http://www.iacajournal.org/index.php/ijca/article/download/132/118.

Dukalskis, A., & Johansen, R. C. (2013). Measuring acceptance of international enforcement of human rights: The United States, Asia, and the International Criminal Court. *Human Rights Quarterly, 35,* 569–597.

Fairlie, M. A. (2011). The United States and the International Criminal Court post-Bush: A beautiful courtship but an unlikely marriage. *Berkeley Journal of International Law, 29,* 528–576.

Falligant, J. (2010). The prosecution of Sudanese President Al Bashir: Why a Security Council deferral would harm the legitimacy of the International Criminal Court. *Wisconsin International Law Journal, 27,* 727–756.

Fernandez de Gurmendi, S. A. (2001). The role of the Prosecutor. In M. Politi & G. Nesi (Eds.), *The Rome Statute of the International Criminal Court: A challenge to impunity* (pp. 55–58). Burlington, VT: Ashgate Dartmouth.

Glasius, M. (2006). *The International Criminal Court: A global civil society achievement.* New York: Routledge.

Grossman, N. (2011). Sex representation on the bench and the legitimacy of international criminal courts. *International Criminal Law Review, 11,* 643–653.

Guariglia, F. (2009). The selection of cases by the office of the prosecutor of the International Criminal Court. In C. Stahn & G. Sluiter (Eds.), *The Emerging Practice of the International Criminal Court* (pp. 209–218). Boston: Martinus Nijhoff Publishers.

Harrington, J., Milde, M., & Vernon, R. (2006). Introduction. In J. Harrington, M. Milde & R. Vernon (Eds.), *Bringing power to justice? The prospects of the International Criminal Court* (pp. 3–25). Ithaca, NY: McGill-Queen's University Press.

Irving, E. (2014). The relationship between the International Criminal Court and its host state: Impact on human rights. *Leiden Journal of International Law, 27,* 479–493.

Kaul, H. P. (2005). Construction site for more justice: The International Criminal Court after two years. *American Journal of International Law, 99,* 370–384.

Lehr-Lehnardt, R. (2002). One small step for women: Female-friendly provisions in the Rome Statute of the International Criminal Court. *Brigham Young University Journal of Public Law, 16,* 317–354.

McGoldrick, D. (2004). Political and legal responses to the ICC. In D. McGoldrick, P. Rowe & E. Donnelly (Eds.), *The permanent International Criminal Court: Legal and policy issues* (pp. 389–452). Portland, OR: Hart Publishing.

Mundis, D. A. (2003). The Assembly of State Parties and the institutional framework of the International Criminal Court. *American Journal of International Law, 97,* 132–147.

Oosterveld, V. (2005). The definition of "gender" in the Rome Statute of the International Criminal Court: A step forward or back for international criminal justice. *Harvard Human Rights Journal, 18,* 55–84.

Ralston, J. H., & Finnin, S. (2008). Investigating international crimes: A review of international law enforcement strategies, expediency versus effectiveness. In D. A. Blumenthal & T. L. H. McCormack (Eds.) The Legacy of Nuremberg: Civilising Influence or Institutionalised Vengeance? Leiden: Martinus Nijhoff Publishers.

Sabharwal, P. (2012). Manifest destiny: The relationship between the United States and the International Criminal Court in a time of upheaval. *New England Journal of International and Comparative Law, 18*, 311–329.

Sadat, L. N. (2000). The evolution of the ICC: From The Hague to Rome and back again. In S. B. Sewall & C. Kaysen (Eds.), *The United States and the International Criminal Court: national security and international law* (pp. 31–50). Lanham, MD: Rowman & Littlefield.

Sadat, L. N. (2011). Avoiding the creation of a gender ghetto in International Criminal Law. *International Criminal Law Review, 11*, 655–662.

Schabas, W. (2007). *An introduction to the International Criminal Court* (3rd ed.). New York: Cambridge University Press.

Stewart, D. (2014). *International criminal law in a nutshell*. St. Paul, MN: West Academic Publishing.

Wald, P. M. (2011). Women on international courts: Some lessons learned. *International Criminal Law Review, 11*, 401–408.

Wippman, D. (2006). Exaggerating the ICC. In J. Harrington, M. Milde & R. Vernon (Eds.), *Bringing power to justice? The prospects of the International Criminal Court* (pp. 99–140). Ithaca, NY: McGill-Queen's University Press.

Chapter 4
Jurisdiction of the Court

Abstract This chapter will describe the jurisdiction of the Court, including the definitions of the crimes to be investigated and the exhaustion of domestic remedies. The Court prosecutes four core crimes: genocide, war crimes, crimes against humanity, and aggression. The Rome Statute reflected an emerging consensus about the first three of these crimes, but deferred agreement on the crime of aggression. Aggression is the most controversial of the four as the definition includes the unlawful use of military force by very senior level military and civilian leaders. The ways in which the Court receives a case will be explored in this chapter, including the UN Security Council referral mechanism, investigations opened by the prosecutor in member states, or cases in which a member country refers a dispute to the Court.

Keywords Ad hoc jurisdiction · Aggression · Complementarity · Core crimes · Crimes against humanity · Customary international law · Deferral · Genocide · Gravity · Natural law · Peremptory norms · *Proprio motu* · Sovereign immunity · Universal jurisdiction · War crimes

4.1 The Concept of Universal Jurisdiction

Trying individuals for international crimes does not necessarily require an international court. Under the doctrine of universal jurisdiction, some international crimes are so serious that any state may exercise jurisdiction over them by prosecuting or extraditing suspects to states willing to prosecute, even absent ordinary jurisdiction. The traditional crimes triggering universal jurisdiction are those where, by convention, all states have an interest in preventing perpetrators from absconding or evading justice, such as piracy on the high seas, slavery, and terrorism. More recently, international treaty regimes established by the Genocide Convention and the Convention Against Torture provide at least minimal obligations on states to prosecute or surrender a suspect to a country that will

© Springer International Publishing Switzerland 2015

A. Novak, *The International Criminal Court*, DOI 10.1007/978-3-319-15832-7_4

prosecute, but these obligations are generally limited to states that have ratified those conventions. Under customary international law, that is, the unwritten code of state practice, certain rules of international state behavior are so fundamental that they apply to all states regardless of their consent to a treaty, as they are rooted in principles of natural law. War crimes are emblematic of these unwritten rules of customary international law: worldwide, states tended to "follow" the laws of war long before international treaties codified these rules. At a minimum, these fundamental rules—known as peremptory norms, and sometimes by the Latin phrase *jus cogens*—include prohibitions on genocide, crimes against humanity, and war crimes. States or individuals that carry out these crimes are always in violation of international law, regardless of whether those crimes are prohibited in national law (Broomhall 2003: 106–110). These peremptory norms are so fundamental that they require states to affirmatively take action to prevent or stop them; the duty on states to outlaw and prosecute these crimes is known by the Latin phrase obligations *erga omnes*. The *jus cogens* nature of genocide makes it the responsibility of every state to prevent and punish the crime, and though not every state has ratified the Genocide Convention, all are bound by the prohibition on genocide as a matter of international customary law (Zhu and Zhang 2011: 175–178).

Notions of universal jurisdiction have bubbled beneath the surface of international politics since World War II. The Nuremberg and Tokyo trials in 1946 were based in part on the concept of universal jurisdiction, as was the capture, trial, and execution of Adolf Eichmann, a Nazi official, in Israel in 1961. In 1998, former Chilean dictator Augusto Pinochet went to London for medical care when Spain requested extradition based on an international arrest warrant for genocide and torture. For the first time, British courts stripped the former head of state of sovereign immunity and allowed prosecution, though Pinochet was eventually released from detention in the United Kingdom due to illness and allowed to return to Chile to face charges. Spain's attempt to try Pinochet for genocide and torture was based on the principle of universal jurisdiction (Findlay et al. 2013: 26). In 2001, Belgium became the first country to domestically prosecute genocide, as four Rwandans were placed on trial for their crimes committed in that country in 1994 (Zhu and Zhang 2011: 178). Similarly, prosecutions of Rwandan perpetrators for genocide have also taken place in Canada, Finland, France, and Switzerland, as these countries were reluctant to extradite the perpetrators due to concerns about the quality of justice in the Rwandan legal system (Kimpimäki 2011: 168, 170–171). More recently, universal jurisdiction is behind efforts to prosecute Hissène Habré, the former dictator of Chad, in a court in Senegal based on an arrest warrant issued in Belgium. Although the International Criminal Court's actual jurisdiction is by no means "universal," the Rome Statute is based on foundational assumptions that some crimes are so serious that they require international prosecution even if they are not specifically prohibited in national law. The goal of the Rome Statute is to create a permanent international forum to prosecute *jus cogens* offenses when domestic systems are unwilling or unable to do so.

4.2 Jurisdiction

The actual jurisdiction that the Court possesses is sharply limited by the negotiated compromises made at the Rome Conference. The International Criminal Court requires three types of jurisdiction in order to initiate a prosecution. It requires (1) subject matter jurisdiction (in the Rome Statute, called *ratione materiae*), (2) jurisdiction over the situation—either personal jurisdiction over the defendant based on nationality (*ratione personae*), or territorial jurisdiction based on the location where the crimes occurred (*ratione loci*)—and (3) jurisdiction in time (*ratione temporis*). To say this more simply, the Court must have jurisdiction over the crime itself, over either the location of the crime or the nationality of the perpetrator (but both are not necessary), and over the period of time in which the crime was committed.

Types of jurisdiction needed to initiate an investigation

Subject matter jurisdiction	Personal jurisdiction	Temporal jurisdiction
Four core crimes: • Genocide • War crimes • Crimes against humanity • Aggression	The crimes must have been committed EITHER: • By a national of a country within the Court's jurisdiction, OR • On the territory of a country within the Court's jurisdiction	The crimes must have been committed on or AFTER: • July 1, 2002, OR • The date on which a country became subject to the Court's jurisdiction (may be retroactive, but not before July 1, 2002)

4.2.1 Subject Matter Jurisdiction

The Court has jurisdiction over four core crimes: genocide, crimes against humanity, war crimes, and aggression. These crimes were in substance largely the same as those pursued at the Nuremberg trials, though "aggression," or the unlawful use of military force, replaced "crimes against peace." In addition to the four core crimes, the Court also has residual authority over crimes that relate to Court's own proceedings. These secondary crimes include contempt of court, perjury or the presentation of false evidence, witness tampering, bribing or retaliating against Court officials, or, in the case of Court officials themselves, soliciting or accepting bribes (Schabas 2007: 140). The Rome Statute does not restrict prosecution to principals: it also permits prosecution for ordering others to commit crimes, including superior direction and command control; aiding and abetting others to commit crimes; and acting in common purpose with other perpetrators. Although the Rome Statute does not specifically outlaw conspiracy to commit crimes, it adopts broad definitions of command responsibility to hold superiors accountable for the acts of their subordinates and common purpose to reach multiple offenders working together (Findlay 2013: 60–61).

   The Court's limited subject matter jurisdiction—essentially confined to the four core crimes—was a negotiated compromise at the Rome Conference.

Caribbean nations objected to the omission of drug trafficking crimes, for instance, and interest in prosecuting terrorism increased after the attacks of September 11, 2001. The difference between the core crimes and offenses such as hijacking, money laundering, or human or drug trafficking is that the latter crimes do not suffer from the same problem of impunity as the core crimes as they are not typically perpetrated by governments themselves or with their complicity, and therefore, perpetrators are not usually shielded from accountability. Any impunity for drug crimes and terrorism is likely the failure of law enforcement rather than the lack of a forum for criminal prosecution. However, many nations at the Rome Conference sought to give the Court subject matter jurisdiction over so-called "treaty crimes" that would allow states to refer criminal situations that violated international treaties to the Court, which would include crimes such as the bombing or hijacking of a civilian aircraft as with the Lockerbie bombing trial. Ultimately, no consensus was reached on this point, and the Court still lacks jurisdiction to prosecute treaty crimes (ibid.: 88–89).

4.2.1.1 Genocide

Genocide is recognized as a uniquely grave crime, both in scale of human atrocity and in its uniquely high intent requirement. The definition of genocide in Article 6 of the Rome Statute is drawn directly from that of the Genocide Convention of 1948: "any of the following acts committed with intent to destroy, in whole or in part, a national, ethnical, racial, or religious group, as such," including killing members of the group; causing serious bodily or mental harm; deliberately inflicting conditions designed to destroy the group in whole or in part; imposing measures to prevent childbirth within the group; or forcibly transferring children of the group to another group. The word "genocide" was coined in 1943 from the Greek word *genos* (race, nation, tribe) and the Latin suffix *–cide* (killing) to describe Nazi atrocities during the Holocaust (Byron 2004: 143). The Genocide Convention, which entered into force in 1951, obligates states to outlaw genocide and take measures to prevent it.

The definition of genocide under the Genocide Convention has not been altered for sixty years. The definition includes a specific intent requirement ("intent to destroy in whole or in part") that creates a high threshold for a perpetrator's mental state. In addition, the offense must be against members of a group with the group, and not the individuals, as the ultimate target. A number of delegates of the Like-Minded Group argued for broadening the 1948 Convention definition of genocide on the basis that it was unnecessarily restrictive, to include, for instance, intent to destroy a culture. The conservative position prevailed because the Genocide Convention's definition was so well-established, though the supporters of a more progressive definition subsequently succeeded in expansively defining "crimes against humanity" to cover situations that fall outside of the definition of genocide (McCormack 2004: 181).

4.2.1.2   Crimes Against Humanity

Unlike the crime of genocide, crimes against humanity have never been codified in a widely accepted treaty, and as a result, negotiations to define the term at the Rome Conference were protracted. As defined in Article 7, crimes against humanity includes any number of specific acts such as murder, extermination, torture, rape, sexual slavery, persecution "when committed as part of a widespread or systematic attack directed against any civilian population, with knowledge of the attack" (Stewart 2014: 129). As stated above, although the Nuremberg and Yugoslavia trials considered "crimes against humanity" to be not entirely distinct from war crimes, the jurisprudence of the Rwanda tribunal made clear that crimes against humanity do not need to take place in armed conflict. The consensus at the Rome Statute completed the separation of the two categories of crimes, and included different elements. Crimes against humanity also include the crime of apartheid, as defined by the Apartheid Convention of 1973, defined as an institutionalized regime of systematic oppression, segregation, and domination of one racial group over another, as was practiced in South Africa between 1948 and 1994.

The definition of crimes against humanity is distinct from the definition of genocide in several ways. Both genocide and crimes against humanity may take place in peacetime or armed conflict and both may be committed by state or non-state actors. Genocide must be targeted at a particular "social, ethnical, racial, or religious group," while crimes against humanity must only affect a "civilian" population. Unlike genocide, crimes against humanity do not require specific intent to destroy a group, only an intent to commit the particular act in question and knowledge of the broader context in which it takes place (Stewart 2014: 206). The Rome Conference also clearly distinguished crimes against humanity from war crimes. Unlike crimes against humanity, war crimes do not need to be part of a widespread or systematic attack on a civilian population, nor do they require official support or knowledge from the government. By contrast, a war crime may constitute only a single incident, but must be carried out during an armed conflict (ibid.: 216). The expansiveness and flexibility of the definition of "crimes against humanity" may make it especially useful in prosecutions to deter future conduct, and the category may subsume the definition of genocide, from which it is only distinguished by a lower intent requirement. Crimes against humanity will often serve as an alternative charge against perpetrators who are also accused of genocide (Murray 2011: 611–615).

4.2.1.3   War Crimes

The definition of war crimes is not as clear and distinct as genocide, as it relates to a broader pattern of conduct occurring during armed conflict, but it is narrower than crimes against humanity as it is, like genocide, largely codified in international treaties. War crimes under the Rome Statute are grouped into two categories: grave breaches of the 1949 Geneva Conventions, and other serious violations of the laws and customs of war. As to the first category, only crimes committed in an international armed conflict and against protected persons (usually non-combatants of the enemy state), as per the Geneva Conventions, fall within the jurisdiction of the Court. Protected persons would include civilians as well as prisoners of war or surrendered enemy troops, but would not include enemy soldiers in combat. The second category is broader, and includes war crimes codified in other international instruments, such as pillage, employing poisoned weapons and asphyxiating gasses, use of exploding or ricocheting bullets, killing a combatant who has surrendered, forced population transfers, scientific experimentation, or attacking buildings of religious, cultural, or historical experience, to name only a few (Venturini 2001: 96–100).

The war crimes clause includes a unique "opt-out" provision in Article 124, which allows any ratifying state to declare that they will not accept the jurisdiction of the Court with regard to war crimes alleged to have been committed by their nationals or on their territories for a period of up to seven years. This is a grave restraint on the Court's jurisdiction, but one that was politically necessary to allow states to accept the Rome Statute without the prospect of surrendering members of their own armed forces in conflicts that were ongoing when the Rome Statute entered into force. In reality, the practical impact of this clause has been marginal, as only two countries have invoked the opt-out clause, France and Colombia; at this point, both of their opt-outs have been lifted or expired. During the Rome Conference, France and the United States expressed concern that the war crimes provisions would fall heavily on their nationals as they were actively involved in many peacekeeping missions overseas (Venturini 2001: 96; Tabak 2009: 1069–1070, 1074).

4.2.1.4 Aggression

The crime of aggression is the successor to the crimes against peace prosecuted at Nuremberg, and generally includes planning, preparation, initiation, or waging of a war of aggression or a war in violation of international treaties. In 1974, the UN General Assembly adopted by consensus a resolution defining aggression as "the use of armed force by a State against the sovereignty, territorial integrity or political independence of another State," including invasion, blockade or bombardment, or military occupation. At the Rome Conference, the negotiating parties agreed that aggression should be included among the core crimes, but they could not reach a consensus on how to define the crime or the role the Security Council should play in determining when it had taken place, as the UN Charter authorizes the Security Council to safeguard UN members from hostile or aggressive war. The Rome Statute left the issue open, providing in Article 5(2) that the crime could be prosecuted once a definition had been adopted and the Statute amended. This was accomplished at the Review Conference held in Kampala, Uganda, in July 2010, and the crime is now defined in the Rome Statute as a new Article 8–*bis* ("bis" meaning "twice," a second Article 8). The actual implementation of this provision was deferred for an additional seven years, to 2017 (Stewart 2014: 219–220).

The United States was a principal opponent of a definition of aggression that could implicate senior political or military officials of *non*-member states, given the extensive military role that the United States plays in humanitarian interventions and other foreign wars. The American delegations to the Assembly of States Parties in 2009 and to the Kampala Review Conference in 2010 were heavily focused on the definition of aggression, and, unlike the initial drafting of the Rome Statute in 1998, the United States found solid support for its position from the four other permanent Security Council members. This united front of major powers was enough to make several significant modifications to the Court's jurisdiction over aggression at the Kampala Review Conference and the resulting amendment (Fairlie 2011: 552–556). Article 8-*bis* as negotiated at Kampala has several distinctive features. First, the definition encompasses both an "act of aggression," which is committed by a state, and a "crime of aggression," which is committed by an individual. An individual cannot be charged with the "crime" of aggression unless the state carries out an "act" of aggression. An individual acting alone without the support of the state cannot be prosecuted—thus, terrorists or insurgents are ineligible. Second, the crime is limited to leaders who exercise control over an armed force; an ordinary soldier cannot be prosecuted. Third, the act of aggression must be a "manifest" violation of the UN Charter, which limits jurisdiction to only the most serious or flagrant cases (Trahan 2011: 55–60). The Kampala compromise also determined that no investigations or prosecutions can take place for aggression until January 1, 2017, and after one year passes following ratification of the amendments by 30 countries.

The Kampala Review Conference also made several important compromises to how the Court would acquire jurisdiction over defendants for purposes of the crime of aggression, which formed the new Article 15-*bis* (state referral and *proprio motu* power) and Article 15-*ter* (Security Council referral). The Kampala Review Conference ultimately created a separate, tailored jurisdictional regime for the crime of aggression that differs from the other three core crimes, sacrificing the Rome Statute's uniformity for the sake of political compromise with the powerful permanent members of the Security Council (Jurdi 2013: 12–14). Article 15-*bis* states that the Court cannot acquire jurisdiction over non-members who are accused of aggression, and allows member states to opt out of jurisdiction over the crime of aggression, to satisfy both the United States (a non-member) and France (a member). For non-members and members that opt out of Article 15-*bis*, a state cannot refer another state for committing a crime of aggression and the Prosecutor may not open a case of her own initiative against that state, which differs from the other core crimes. In addition, the Court can only acquire jurisdiction based on state referral or prosecutorial initiative if the Security Council has not acted on the act of aggression within six months, a "filter" mechanism to require Security Council involvement. Article 15-*ter* confirms that the Security Council essentially has the first option to determine whether an act of aggression occurred and to grant the Court jurisdiction (Trahan 2011: 82–85). However, some scholars have suggested that giving the Security Council such a prominent role over the jurisdiction of the crime of aggression compromises the Court's autonomy and subordinates the universal nature of international law to major power interests. The increased role of the Security Council in prosecutions for aggression reflects the highly political nature of the crime (Trotter 2012: 360).

Essential elements of the four core crimes

Genocide	• Specific intent to destroy a national, ethnic, racial, or religious group as such
	• Includes killing, causing serious bodily or mental harm, imposing conditions on group with intent to destroy, preventing births, or forcibly transferring children
Crimes against humanity	• Acts committed as part of a widespread or systematic attack
	• Directed against any civilian population
	• Pursuant to a government or organizational policy to commit the attack (thus not an isolated incident)
	• Perpetrator must have knowledge of the nature of the attack (lower intent than genocide)
War crimes	• Must occur during armed conflict
	• Does not need to be widespread or systematic, or pursuant to a government policy
	• Victims generally must be "protected persons," which include civilians and surrendered troops, but not other combatants
Aggression	• Planning, preparation, initiation, or execution of an act of aggressive war in violation of the UN Charter
	• By a person who exercises control over a state's military force
	• "Acts of aggression" include invasion, blockade, bombardment, or occupation

4.2.2 Personal or Territorial Jurisdiction

The Court may only consider cases involving allegations of the four core crimes if they were committed (1) within the territory of a state party to the Rome Statute (territorial jurisdiction), or (2) by a national of a state party (personal jurisdiction). The Court cannot consider cases involving non-parties *unless* the situation is referred to the Prosecutor by the Security Council or a non-party state specifically requests the Court to investigate its own territory or nationals pursuant to Article 12, known as ad hoc jurisdiction (Stewart 2014: 133). Ad hoc jurisdiction is a type of voluntary self-referral by a *non*-member state. All prosecutions to date have been based solely on territory and not nationality. This is true even in the cases where the Security Council referred situations involving non-members such as Libya and Sudan; those referrals did not include crimes committed by Libyan or Sudan nationals on the territories of *other* non-member states (Schabas 2007: 71–72, 75–76). As explained below, however, even if these criteria are satisfied, personal jurisdiction may nonetheless be extended to government officials acting in their official capacities as there is no sovereign immunity; on the other hand, it will not be established over corporations, persons without the capacity for criminal responsibility, or those under 18 years of age at the time of the crime. The Rome Statute has no provision for *in absentia* proceedings. Defendants must be taken into custody and turned over by states themselves.

4.2.2.1 Sovereign Immunity

Under international law, diplomats, heads of state, foreign ministers, and other senior state officials typically have immunity from prosecution when in foreign countries, although this immunity attaches only to the office and not to the person, and may allow prosecution when an officeholder leaves his or her position. In addition, international law recognizes immunity from prosecution for official acts of state, and attaches to any person acting on behalf of the government. The Rome Statute sharply curtails these traditional immunities for the purpose of prosecuting international crimes. The official position of alleged perpetrators does not exempt them from individual responsibility for acts that are crimes under international law. The Torture Convention prohibiting official or state-sanctioned torture and the Geneva Conventions prohibiting war crimes committed in international armed conflict both remove traditional immunities for state officials. The Rome Statute does as well (Akande 2006: 47–55).

4.2.2.2 Natural Persons Over Age 18

The Rome Statute permits prosecution only of natural persons—that is, human beings—and not of legal persons, despite an effort by the Preparatory Committee to punish corporations and other organizations that may have been complicit in or that profited from human rights abuses. This is different from the Nuremberg trials, where membership in a criminal organization was prosecuted. The Rome Statute's definitions of the four core crimes include attempted crimes and direct and public incitement of genocide. In addition, the Court does not permit jurisdiction over any person who was under the age of 18 at the time the alleged crime was committed. This was to ensure consistency with international law, such as the Convention on the Rights of the Child and its protocols relating to child soldiers (Kim 2003: 308–311). Under the Rome Statute and international law, child soldiers are victims themselves, and to the extent that they are also perpetrators, criminal liability falls on those adults who recruit them and direct their actions. The Statute also criminalizes official and command responsibility; this means, that a superior may be liable for the crimes of subordinates, even if the principal is a head of state or government, an elected representative, a government official, or a senior military leader where the superior knew or should have known that grave crimes were being committed and failed to take all necessary and reasonable measures to stop them (ibid.: 310–313).

4.2.3 Temporal Jurisdiction

Besides personal jurisdiction over the defendant and subject matter jurisdiction over the crimes, the Court requires a third type of jurisdiction: jurisdiction in time. Under Article 11 of the Rome Statute, the Court only has jurisdiction over crimes committed after the Statute entered into force, which was July 1, 2002. In addition, the Court only has jurisdiction to prosecute crimes once it otherwise establishes personal jurisdiction, such as after a state party ratifies the Rome Statute or the Security Council refers jurisdiction over a non-party to the Prosecutor, unless the state party or the Security Council specifically authorize retroactive jurisdiction—but never before July 1, 2002 (Cameron 2004: 70). So far, three ratifying states have given the Court retroactive jurisdiction: Côte d'Ivoire, which, in 2003, gave retroactive jurisdiction over crimes committed since September 19, 2002, to encompass its recent civil war; Palestine, which upon attempted ratification in 2009 gave the Court retroactive jurisdiction to back to the establishment of the Court on July 1, 2002; and Ukraine, which in April 2014 gave the Court retroactive jurisdiction for the period from November 21, 2013, to February 22, 2014, to encompass the government's crackdowns on democracy protestors before the Russian invasion of the Crimea. However, the Court has not recognized jurisdiction over Palestine before November 29, 2012, the date on which the UN General Assembly reclassified Palestine as a non-member observer state and therefore eligible to ratify the Rome Statute. On December 31, 2014, Palestine acceded to the Rome Statute, which will raise many difficult questions about Palestine's temporal jurisdiction. The case of Palestine is explored later in this book in Chap. 7 (Statement of the Prosecutor, September 2, 2014; Rudoren 2015).

The Court's temporal jurisdictional limits raise questions about "continuing" situations, namely those that began before July 1, 2002, or the date of ratification by a state party, but continued into the period over which the Court has jurisdiction. Is the Court precluded from considering crimes that were underway at the time the Statute entered into force? What if the harm of those crimes was not felt until afterward? The trial chamber at the Rwanda tribunal explicitly approved the application of the doctrine of "continuing crime" to the crime of conspiracy to commit genocide or crimes against humanity, so long as the conspiracy continued into the relevant period over which the tribunal had jurisdiction. Certainly, a common criminal plan could have been agreed upon before the Statute entered into force, and then subsequently executed or completed (Stahn et al. 2005: 429–430). Although the Court has not faced such a situation, it is probable that the Court would interpret its temporal jurisdiction expansively, as the Rwanda tribunal did with conspiracy to commit genocide when that conspiracy predated the time frame of the tribunal's statute.

4.3 Triggering Jurisdiction Under the Rome Statute

Because the International Criminal Court has global reach and must selectively choose the cases that it investigates, jurisdiction is not pre-defined or automatic. The Rome Statute authorizes three ways in which the jurisdiction of the Court may be triggered. First, a government may refer a situation to the Court involving its own territory or its own nationals; the government does not need to be a state party to the Rome Statute so long as it consents to the Court's jurisdiction on a situational basis. Second, the UN Security Council may refer a case to the Prosecutor, even over non-member states, in the interests of international peace and security. Finally, and most controversially, the Prosecutor may open an investigation into a state party on her own initiative. This is known as the Prosecutor's *proprio motu* authority.

4.3.1 State Party Referral

A state party to the Rome Statute may refer to the Court a situation involving its own nationals or its own territory. Critics of the Rome Statute believed that post-conflict regimes would be reluctant to enter into the Statute or otherwise trigger the Court's jurisdiction, but the Court's actual experience has seen a growing number of ratifications from conflict-prone or post-conflict countries over the last few years, including self-referrals by Uganda, Democratic Republic of the Congo, and Central African Republic. Although the drafters at the Rome Conference intended for governments to be able to refer each other to the Court, it was completely unexpected—and indeed, quite astonishing—that the first cases submitted to the Court were *self*-referrals of internal conflicts. Self-referral has been approved by the Pre-Trial Chamber, but the "one-sided" nature of the investigations against rebel leaders only and not against government officials has caused some concern among human rights activists. The consequence of self-referral is that it ensures that a situation will be pursued by the Court, rather than simply falling within the Prosecutor's discretion to open a case (Schabas 2007: 143–150).

Article 12(3) of the Rome Statute allows a state that is not a party to the Rome Statute to accept the jurisdiction of the Court by way of a declaration lodged with the Registrar: this is known as ad hoc jurisdiction. Article 12(3) goes beyond self-referral: it allows *non-parties* to submit to the jurisdiction of the Court crimes that were committed on their territories or by their nationals. The rationale for Article 12(3) is to extend the Statute's scope by offering states that are not parties to the Statute the opportunity to accept the Court's jurisdiction on an ad hoc or situational basis without putting non-party states under pressure to accede to the Statute itself. Unlike self-referrals by members, however, ad hoc referrals are limited in scope. Unlike a member's self-referral, filing an Article 12(3) declaration does not place any obligation on the Prosecutor to pursue the case; it is only a "precondition" to the exercise of jurisdiction and does not itself trigger an investigation.

The Court must decide whether to accept ad hoc jurisdiction, and the Prosecutor is not obliged to begin the investigative process. In any event, the Pre-Trial Chamber must give the Prosecutor prior authorization for the commencement of any investigation (Stahn et al. 2005: 421–424). The Rome Statute has not yet had to deal with difficult questions concerning the creation of new states or the dissolution of old states, but membership in the International Criminal Court regime may change depending on secession or merger, transfer of territory, or other boundary changes. These changes may alter jurisdiction over territory or a perpetrator's nationality, and may affect the Court's jurisdiction in time, an important consideration for the special case of Palestine (Wills 2014: 428–435).

4.3.2 United Nations Security Council Referral

The second means of triggering the exercise of jurisdiction by the Court is through a referral by the UN Security Council. Composed of 15 members, five permanent and ten elected from the General Assembly for two year terms, the Security Council requires nine votes to adopt a resolution without a veto from one of the five permanent members (United States, United Kingdom, Russia, China, and France). Under the Relationship Agreement between the United Nations and the International Criminal Court, the Security Council is not to refer cases that do not otherwise fall within the Court's jurisdiction, such as crimes that were committed before July 1, 2002. Since the International Criminal Court is not a UN organ, the Rome Statute requires that the UN pay the expenses related to cases referred to the Court by the Security Council. However, when the Security Council referred the situation in Darfur Province, Sudan, to the Court over a United States abstention, the United States refused to allow the UN to pay. Instead, the text of the Darfur referral (Resolution 1593) required that states parties to the Rome Statute and other voluntary contributors pay for the case, one of the diplomatic concessions in the referral. Simply because the Security Council refers a situation to the Prosecutor, however, does not require her to open an investigation or prosecute if insufficient evidence exists. The Darfur referral shows the influence that the United States, a non-party, possesses over the Court's operations, but the Darfur referral—and the decision not to veto the resolution—signaled a marked shift in the previously hostile American policy toward the Court (Schabas 2007: 153–158; Philips 1999: 73; Heyder 2006: 659).

4.3.3 Proprio Motu Power

By far the most controversial trigger mechanism at the Rome Conference was the ability of the Prosecutor to open an investigation of her own accord, known as the *proprio motu* power, as defined at Article 15 of the Rome Statute. The

Like-Minded Group made the independence of the Prosecutor to initiate a case one of the main planks of the negotiations, and the *proprio motu* power was perhaps the provision most vigorously opposed by the United States. Unlike her counterparts at other international criminal tribunals, the ICC Prosecutor must secure the approval of the Pre-Trial Chamber under Article 15 of the Rome Statute before initiating criminal investigations of her own motion. In this way, although the Prosecutor has broad discretion to select situations, she actually has less unchecked power compared to the prosecutors at the Rwanda and Yugoslavia tribunals. If the Prosecutor concludes that a reasonable basis exists to proceed with an investigation, she must submit a request for authorization and any supporting material to the Pre-Trial Chamber. Supporting material is provided to the judges, and victims are able to make presentations to the Chamber at this stage. Submissions to the Prosecutor for candidate situations to investigate may come from the UN, intergovernmental organizations, NGOs, individuals, or groups; the Office of the Prosecutor received nearly 2,000 communications from more than 100 countries in the first three years of the Court's operations. If the Prosecutor determines that a case is not worth pursuing, she must provide this information to the requestor, but her decision is not appealable (Schabas 2007: 160–166).

One of the most controversial aspects of the International Criminal Court's work is its need to decide which situations and cases to prosecute, as the Court is limited to prosecuting a handful of cases out of thousands of potential situations. Although the Prosecutor does not control all case selection before the Court—she shares that responsibility with the Security Council, other member states, and the judges of the Pre-Trial Chamber—the exercise of her *proprio motu* power in selecting cases to prosecute is nonetheless the clearest expression of the Court's goals and priorities. The current Prosecutor, Fatou Bensouda, and her predecessor Luis Moreno Ocampo both relied on the concept of "gravity" in selecting cases, choosing what they perceived were the worst of the worst, and justified their selections through appeals to impartial and objective criteria (deGuzman 2012: 269, 271, 274). As explained below, however, the Rome Statute does not require that the Court prosecute only the *worst* or *most serious* cases; rather, the cases simply need to pass a threshold of seriousness, i.e., they must be serious *enough* to warrant prosecution. While all prosecutors, both international and domestic, must make difficult decisions of cases to prosecute, the global reach of the ICC and its very limited resources make case selection a particularly important aspect of the Court's work.

4.4 Admissibility

Not every crime falling within the Court's jurisdiction may be prosecuted. Where the available information provides a reasonable basis to believe that a crime has been committed that falls within the Court's jurisdiction, the next step is to consider whether the case is admissible. Admissibility requires two components:

complementarity and gravity. The complementarity principle requires that the Court defer to national prosecutions, and it may only prosecute where a state is unwilling or unable to do so. The gravity principle requires that the crimes committed be of a sufficient scale or severity to warrant prosecution before an international tribunal. To proceed, the Prosecutor must satisfy both criteria for admissibility (Guariglia 2009: 214). Even if a case is admissible, the Rome Statute provides that the UN Security Council may suspend an investigation or a prosecution for a renewable one-year period, known as the deferral power. Whether the Prosecutor may proceed with a case—in other words, whether she has met the criteria for jurisdiction and admissibility—is subject to a majority vote of the judges of the Pre-Trial Chamber.

4.4.1 Complementarity

One of the most essential aspects of International Criminal Court jurisdiction is the principle of complementarity, permitting Court prosecutions only where a country is unwilling or unable to do so. The complementarity principle was the International Criminal Court's response to the criticisms of the ICTY and ICTR that international trials were insufficiently sensitive to local realities and justice processes (Raub 2009: 1019). Holding trials in the country where alleged crimes were committed has a number of advantages: evidence is more readily available, costs associated with investigation and procurement of witnesses are minimized, and most of all, the proceedings have the greatest legitimacy and impact for their most important audiences. Thus, they have the greatest potential for promoting reconciliation and restoring the social balance in a post-conflict situation (Broomhall 2003: 84). A distant tribunal in The Hague, by contrast, is in a less advantageous position when it comes to investigating and prosecuting a crime. Some observers have called on the Office of the Prosecutor to engage in *proactive* complementarity by encouraging and assisting national governments to prosecute international crimes, as this would help end impunity for offenders with limited resources and fit within the logic of the Rome Statute's complementarity principle (Burke-White 2008: 55–56). The risk is double-sided: just as a government complicit in serious crimes may try to use legal proceedings to give itself immunity, so too might a new government prosecute former regime officials in an unfair way and subject them to harsh punishment. How strongly the Court respects (or should respect) domestic proceedings remains to be seen.

The Preamble and Article 1 of the Rome Statute declare that the ICC is to be "complementary" to national jurisdictions, a notion that had overwhelming support at the Rome Conference. As defined by the Rome Statute, the complementarity principle requires that the Prosecutor must notify all states parties that she has determined that a "reasonable basis" exists to commence an investigation. Under Article 18, if a state responds within one month that it is investigating the criminal acts and the alleged perpetrators, the Prosecutor must defer to that state's investigation unless the Pre-Trial Chamber otherwise authorizes. This Article—proposed by the United States—significantly limits the ability of the Prosecutor to initiate cases, but it does not apply in the event of a Security Council referral (Broomhall 2003: 87). It appears that the burden of proof that a state is unwilling or unable to prosecute is on the Prosecutor, which may place her in the awkward position of attacking a state party's judicial process or good faith. However, to prevent impunity for offenders, the Court itself, and not the state party, is the final arbiter of whether a domestic proceeding is sufficient (Nsereko 1999: 117–118).

Article 17 of the Rome Statute lays out the substance of admissibility. A case cannot be prosecuted if it is being investigated or prosecuted by a state with jurisdiction, unless the state is unwilling or unable to "genuinely" proceed. Under the Rome Statute, the decision as to whether a national investigation is genuine and should preempt prosecution by the Court is subject to a majority vote of the Pre-Trial Chamber. In addition, a case cannot be prosecuted if it was investigated by a state and the state has decided not to prosecute—unless its failure to prosecute was not genuine. A person cannot be tried for conduct for which he or she has already been tried, unless that trial was for the purpose of shielding that person from criminal responsibility or was not conducted in a manner consistent with international due process norms. The Court itself makes the determination whether or not a national prosecution is "genuine." Although the delegates to the Rome Conference did not want a Court that could review national decisions, they also realized the danger in allowing national authorities to "block" ICC prosecutions, one of the central compromises of the Rome Statute (Struett 2008: 124). One of the consequences of the complementarity principle is that the Court can only prosecute the *unprosecuted*, and the complementarity principle requires the Prosecutor to scrutinize a country's transitional justice efforts at a broader level. Although the structure of the Court was designed to minimize political influences on Prosecutorial decision-making, Greenawalt (2007: 629–633) has argued that the Prosecutor's discretion to determine whether a national prosecution is genuine is a complex political calculation.

The complementarity principle makes the International Criminal Court a court of last resort. The Court only has jurisdiction if there is evidence that national authorities are attempting to shield the accused from accountability for grave crimes. This is in contrast to the Yugoslav and Rwanda tribunals, which had primacy over national courts (Mendes 2010: 26). What if the only way to end an armed conflict is for a state to provide immunity from prosecution for former combatants? The Rome Statute does not expressly allow such an exception for amnesties, especially when they potentially provide impunity for serious crimes. The Prosecutor or the Pre-Trial Chamber may decide that testifying before a South African-style truth and reconciliation commission in exchange for amnesty, for instance, is a sufficiently "genuine" investigation to satisfy Article 17 (Broomhall 2003: 101). Colombia presents a variation on this theme. If the Court is to intervene in Colombia, it will need to delve into the issue of complementarity with the

Justice and Peace Law of 2005, which allows greatly reduced sentences (though not amnesties from punishment) for left-wing and right-wing paramilitary groups who are suspected in genocide, crimes against humanity, or war crimes. The Court has not stated definitively whether these reduced alternative sentences are respectful enough of the Rome Statute's standard for admissibility (Ambos 2010: 3–4; Bueno and Rozas 2013: 230).

The crime of aggression poses a unique challenge for the concept of complementarity. Because aggression requires a state to commit an act of aggression before an individual can be prosecuted for the crime of aggression, the complementarity provision would seem to require that the state have an opportunity to prosecute its leaders for the state's own aggression before the International Criminal Court can investigate, even if the Security Council finds the act of aggression to violate international peace and security. In essence, if a state's leaders committed the act of aggression, it would seem odd that they would ever prosecute themselves for their own violation; on the other hand, if a state's leaders are replaced, complementarity fails to protect the former leaders' due process rights against overzealous or vindictive prosecutions for acts of state. The principle of complementarity was designed to prevent the problem of "sham" prosecutions that provide immunity to offenders; it may be an imperfect tool to combat the opposite problem, where courts are "all too willing" to prosecute and fail to provide due process assurances (Trahan 2012: 572). The Rome Statute provides little guidance for domestic prosecutions of aggression. As noted above, the Court does not have jurisdiction over non-members for the crime of aggression, but this may not stop other member states from attempting to prosecute those perpetrators in domestic courts. The crime of aggression also diverges from the Rome Statute's provisions for victim involvement, since the "victim" is a state and not an individual (Jurdi 2013: 14–19; Trahan 2012: 587).

4.4.2 Gravity

The ICC does not have the resources or will to punish every violator of international criminal law. Although any crime falling within the jurisdiction of the Court is a serious matter, the Rome Statute also requires the Prosecutor to determine that a crime is of sufficient gravity to justify further action by the Court. The Office of the Prosecutor has in the past expressly refused to open an investigation due to the lack of sufficient gravity, including crimes committed by British soldiers in Iraq, as the United Kingdom is a state party to the Rome Statute (though Iraq is not). According to the Prosecutor, British soldiers in Iraq were responsible for no more than 20 deaths that could constitute war crimes, of insufficient gravity compared to the other serious cases pending before the Court. The Prosecutor must consider the scale and nature of the crimes and the manner in which they were committed in making a determination as to whether a crime meets the "gravity" requirement (Guariglia 2009:

213–214). An element of the "gravity" requirement is that prosecutions fall on senior leaders or those most responsible, rather than foot soldiers or low-level perpetrators. Senior leaders are those most likely to avoid accountability for their crimes; at the same time, their prosecution is likely to have the strongest deterrent effect (Schabas 2007: 243). Heller (2009) has argued that simply counting the number of deaths is only part of the "gravity" analysis: the Court should also look to whether the crimes were systematic or part of a broader policy; whether they cause "social alarm" in the international community; and whether they were committed by states or by non-state actors. The gravity threshold for admissibility looks to the severity of the situation as a whole, not to whether an individual perpetrator's crimes are severe enough to meet the definitions of the core crimes. Some scholars refer to the overall gravity threshold for admissibility as "situational gravity" to distinguish it from the seriousness of a perpetrator's specific crimes (Waschefort 2014).

It is important to emphasize that the Rome Statute does not require that the Prosecutor prosecute the most serious crimes; rather, the Prosecutor may only prosecute crimes that reach a certain threshold of seriousness. The Prosecutor's statements that she selects only the most culpable perpetrators of the most serious crimes is different than the Rome Statute's gravity threshold; rather, these statements reflect her prosecutorial discretion (deGuzman 2012: 286–287). DeGuzman (2008: 1403) has distinguished between the objective "gravity" threshold required by the Rome Statute and the "relative gravity" judgment that the Prosecutor makes in selecting from among the cases that surpass the threshold. Indeed, the Prosecutor may have good reasons to go after mid-level or less senior officials, as these cases may be less complex and may help build up a body of evidence that could be used to implicate and prosecute more senior officials. Trials against senior heads of state or military leaders are among the most complex that the Court will face; lower-level convictions, established facts, and preexisting testimony might benefit leadership prosecutions, especially for the crime of aggression (Drumbl 2009: 315).

So far, the Pre-Trial Chamber has been inclined to require only minimal gravity for admissibility beyond what is inherent in the Rome Statute's provisions regarding jurisdiction, such as the requirement of crimes against humanity that they be widespread and systematic (deGuzman 2013: 477). The Prosecutor's decision not to investigate potential British war crimes in Iraq on the grounds that the crimes did not meet the "severity" threshold is not easy to square with the decision of the Court to prosecute Thomas Lubanga for conscription and enlistment of child soldiers in the Democratic Republic of the Congo. Although the Prosecutor argued that such soldiers were responsible for thousands of deaths, Lubanga was not charged with murder. The Pre-Trial Chamber ultimately accepted the Lubanga case as sufficiently grave, though human rights observers criticized the Prosecutor for not bring more expansive charges. In ruling on the admissibility of the Lubanga case, the Pre-Trial Chamber ruled that the recruitment of child soldiers caused "social alarm" in the international community and met the severity requirement (Schabas 2007: 240–241). As deGuzman (2013:

480–485) writes, the Pre-Trial Chamber has at times emphasized the quantitative and at other times the qualitative; it found, for instance, that a defendant in the situation in Darfur, Sudan, Bahar Idress Abu Garda, met the gravity threshold for an attack that killed twelve peacekeepers and wounded eight others, a relatively low number of direct victims. She agrees with the judges that the gravity threshold should be minimal; to the extent that the Court should impose a minimal severity threshold for prosecution, the judges should consider this by using the Court's subject matter jurisdiction (for instance, whether an incident qualifies as a crime against humanity), rather than through the ambiguous notion of gravity (ibid. 2013: 485).

4.5 Deferral by the UN Security Council

In establishing a powerful independent prosecutor, the Rome Statute sought to limit the possibilities for political interference with the Court, and especially on prosecutorial decision-making. Although the five permanent Security Council members sought a way to veto ICC prosecutions, the consensus at the Rome Conference was that allowing a veto over prosecutions would lead, in practice, to impunity for offenders. The result was another compromise. Chapter 7 of the UN Charter tasks the Security Council with deciding which measures are necessary to maintain international peace and security. The Rome Statute balances respect for the Security Council's role with the need to maintain the independence of the Court prosecutor, by allowing the Council to suspend any investigation or prosecution for a renewable period of 12 months by passing a Security Council resolution. This is the Security Council's deferral power. However, a veto by any of the five permanent members can prevent the initial suspension or subsequent renewals (Brown 2000: 76).

In 2002, the UN Security Council invoked Article 16 of the Rome Statute by requesting that the Court not commence a case against any personnel in a UN peacekeeping operation from a non-party state for a 12 month renewable period beginning July 1, 2002. The resolution resulted from concern of the United States that American nationals faced legal exposure as UN peacekeepers, and the United States threatened to veto all future peacekeeping missions unless the Council agreed to shield UN peacekeepers from prosecution. The 12-month deferral was controversial because it was intended to be perpetually renewed, though in the actual event it was only renewed once before expiring after serious international criticism arose over American treatment of Iraqi nationals at Abu Ghraib prison. This debate was unexpected, because the purpose of Article 16 was to defer prosecutions of certain situations in order to benefit peace processes or other resolutions and to allow national officials time to launch their own criminal proceedings, not to shield categories of persons from prosecution (Schabas 2007: 168–169; Falligant 2010: 743).

4.6 Discussion Questions

1. Although the United States is not a party, in what ways did the United States shape the ultimate text of the Rome Statute? Do you think these aspects of the Court's jurisdiction will be sufficient to bring the United States into the ICC family in the future?
2. What are the relative risks and advantages to having a strong, independent prosecutor? Of having a strong role for the UN Security Council?

4.7 Further Reading

Students interested in the crime of aggression may be interested in a new book by Carrie McDougall, *The Crime of Aggression under the Rome Statute of the International Criminal Court* (Cambridge University Press 2013). The book includes a comprehensive introduction to the crime of aggression, including the definition and jurisdictional limitations negotiated at the Kampala Review Conference, and assesses the potential for prosecutions after the amendments enter into force. In addition, two recent books from Cambridge University Press provide sophisticated overviews of the Court's territorial jurisdiction and the principle of complementarity: Michail Vagias, *The Territorial Jurisdiction of the International Criminal Court* (Cambridge University Press 2014) and Carsen Stahn and Mohamed M. El Zeidy, *The International Criminal Court and Complementarity: From Theory to Practice* (Cambridge University Press 2011). Both books comprehensively address many of the questions raised in this chapter about the Court's jurisdiction and the admissibility of a case. For an expert analysis of the Court's triggering procedure, see Héctor Olásolo, *The Triggering Procedure of the International Criminal Court* (Brill 2003).

References

Akande, D. (2006). The application of international law immunities in prosecutions for international crimes. In J. Harrington, M. Milde & R. Vernon (Eds.), *Bringing power to justice? The prospects of the international criminal court* (pp. 47–98). Ithaca, NY: McGill-Queen's University Press.

Ambos, K. (2010). *The Colombian peace process and the principle of complementarity of the International Criminal Court*. New York: Springer.

Broomhall, B. (2003). *International justice and the International Criminal Court: Between sovereignty and the rule of law*. New York: Oxford University Press.

Brown, B. (2000). The statute of the ICC: Past, present, and future. In S. B. Sewell & C. Kaysen (Eds.), *The United States and the International Criminal Court: National security and international law* (pp. 61–84). Lanham, MD: Rowman & Littlefield.

Bueno, I. & Rozas, A. D. (2013). Which approach to justice in Colombia under the era of the ICC. In D. L. Rothe, J. Meernik & P. Ingadottir (Eds.), *The realities of international criminal justice* (pp. 211–248). Boston: Martinus Nijhoff Publishers.

Burke-White, W. W. (2008). Proactive complementarity: The International Criminal Court and national courts in the Rome system of international justice. *Harvard International Law Journal, 49*, 53–108.

Byron, C. (2004). The crime of genocide. In D. McGoldrick, P. Rowe & E. Donnelly (Eds.), *The permanent International Criminal Court: Legal and policy issues* (pp. 143–178). Portland, OR: Hart Publishing.

Cameron, I. (2004). Jurisdiction and admissibility issues under the ICC Statute. In D. McGoldrick, P. Rowe & E. Donnelly (Eds.), *The permanent International Criminal Court: Legal and policy issues* (pp. 65–94). Portland, OR: Hart Publishing.

deGuzman, M. M. (2008). Gravity and the legitimacy of the International Criminal Court. *Fordham International Law Journal, 32*, 1400–1465.

deGuzman, M. M. (2012). Choosing to prosecute: Expressive selection at the International Criminal Court. *Michigan Journal of International Law, 33*, 265–320.

deGuzman, M. M. (2013). The International Criminal Court's gravity jurisprudence at ten. *Washington University Global Studies Law Review, 12*, 475–486.

Drumbl, M. A. (2009). The push to criminalize aggression: Something lost amid the gains? *Case Western Reserve International Law Journal, 41*, 291–319.

Fairlie, M. A. (2011). The United States and the International Criminal Court post-Bush: A beautiful courtship but an unlikely marriage. *Berkeley Journal of International Law, 29*, 528–576.

Falligant, J. (2010). The prosecution of Sudanese president Al Bashir: Why a Security Council deferral would harm the legitimacy of the International Criminal Court. *Wisconsin International Law Journal, 27*, 727–756.

Findlay, M., Kuo, L. B., & Wei, L. S. (2013). *International and comparative criminal justice: A critical introduction*. New York: Routledge.

Greenawalt, A. K. A. (2007). Justice without politics: Prosecutorial discretion and the International Criminal Court. *New York University Journal of International Law and Politics, 39*, 583–673.

Guariglia, F. (2009). The selection of cases by the office of the prosecutor of the International Criminal Court. In C. Stahn & G. Sluiter (Eds.), *The emerging practice of the International Criminal Court* (pp. 209–218). Boston: Martinus Nijhoff Publishers.

Heller, K. J. (2009). Situational gravity under the Rome Statute. In C. Stahn & L. van den Herik (Eds.), *Future perspectives on international criminal justice*. The Hague: TMC Asser Press.

Heyder, C. (2006). The UN Security Council's referral of the crimes in Darfur to the International Criminal Court in light of US opposition to the Court: Implications for the International Criminal Court's functions and status. *Berkeley Journal of International Law, 24*, 650–671.

Jurdi, N. N. (2013). The domestic prosecution of the crime of aggression after the International Criminal Court Review Conference: Possibilities and alternatives. *Melbourne Journal of International Law, 14*, 1–20.

Kim, Y. S. (2003). *The International Criminal Court: A commentary of the Rome Statute*. Leeds, UK: Wisdom House.

Kimpimäki, M. (2011). Genocide in Rwanda—is it really Finland's concern? *International Criminal Law Review, 11*, 155–176.

McCormack, T. L. H. (2004). Crimes against humanity. In D. McGoldrick, P. Rowe & E. Donnelly (Eds.), *The permanent International Criminal Court: Legal and policy issues* (pp. 179–202). Portland, OR: Hart Publishing.

Mendes, E. (2010). *Peace and justice at the International Criminal Court: A court of last resort*. Northampton, MA: Edward Elgar.

Murray, A. R. J. (2011). Does international law still require a "crime of crimes"? A comparative review of genocide and crimes against humanity. *Goettingen Journal of International Law, 3*, 598–615.

Nsereko, D. D. N. (1999). The International Criminal Court: Jurisdictional and related issues. *Criminal Law Forum, 10,* 87–120.

Philips, R. B. (1999). The International Criminal Court statute: Jurisdiction and admissibility. *Criminal Law Forum, 10,* 61–85.

Raub, L. (2009). Positioning hybrid tribunals in international criminal justice. *New York University Journal of International Law and Politics, 41,* 1013–1053.

Rudoren, J. (2015, January 1). Joining International Criminal Court wouldn't guarantee Palestine a war crimes case. *New York Times,* http://www.nytimes.com/2015/01/02/world/middleeast/court-membership-wouldnt-guarantee-palestinians-a-war-crimes-case.html

Schabas, W. (2007). *An introduction to the International Criminal Court* (3rd ed.). New York: Cambridge University Press.

Stahn, C., El Zeidy, M. M. E., & Olásolo, H. (2005). The International Criminal Court's ad hoc jurisdiction revisited. *American Journal of International Law, 99,* 421–431.

Stewart, D. (2014). *International criminal law in a nutshell.* St. Paul, MN: West Academic Publishing.

Struett, M. J. (2008). *The politics of constructing the International Criminal Court: NGOs, discourse, and agency.* New York: Palgrave Macmillan.

Tabak, S. (2009). Article 124, war crimes, and the development of the Rome Statute. *Georgetown Journal of International Law, 40,* 1069–1099.

Trahan, J. (2011). The Rome Statute's amendment on the crime of aggression: Negotiations at the Kampala Review Conference. *International Criminal Law Review, 11,* 49–104.

Trahan, J. (2012). Is complementarity the right approach for the International Criminal Court's crime of aggression? Considering the problem of "overzealous" national court prosecutions. *Cornell International Law Journal, 45,* 569–601.

Trotter, A. (2012). Of aggression and diplomacy: The Security Council, the International Criminal Court, and *jus ad bellum. New England Journal of International and Comparative Law, 18,* 351–367.

Venturini, G. (2001). War crimes in international armed conflicts. In M. Politi & G. Nesi (Eds.), *The Rome Statute of the International Criminal Court: A challenge to impunity* (pp. 95–106). Burlington, VT: Ashgate Dartmouth.

Waschefort, G. (2014). Gravity as a requirement in international criminal prosecutions: Implications for South African courts. *Comparative and International Law Journal of Southern Africa, 47,* 38–63.

Wills, A. (2014). Old crimes, new states and the temporal jurisdiction of the International Criminal Court. *Journal of International Criminal Justice, 12,* 407–435.

Zhu, W., & Zhang, B. (2011). Expectation of prosecuting the crimes of genocide in China. In R. Provost & P. Akhavan (Eds.), *Confronting genocide* (pp. 173–194). New York: Springer.

Chapter 5
Investigation and Prosecution

Abstract This chapter will provide an overview of the investigatory and adjudicatory process at the International Criminal Court, including the gathering of evidence, witness protection, and the mechanics of the trial process. The chapter will also summarize the nine situations currently under investigation. The challenges of controlling the investigation of an uncooperative government, as well as the special obstacles faced by defense counsel are included. The role that victims play in criminal proceedings is an additional emphasis of this chapter. As an effort to promote the restorative goals of the transitional and post-conflict justice movement, victims have legal representation and a formal role in the trial proceeding.

Keywords Arrest · Criminal procedure · Defense bar · *In absentia* · Rules of procedure and evidence · Witness protection

5.1 The Indictments

After an investigation has commenced, the Prosecutor may seek from the Pre-Trial Chamber a warrant of arrest or summons to appear. The Rome Statute does not use the term "indictment," as in a common law system, but rather "document containing the charges." The Pre-Trial Chamber must be satisfied that there are reasonable grounds to believe that the person has committed a crime within the Court's jurisdiction, and that the person's arrest is necessary. The Court may also issue a summons for a person to appear, which will avoid arrest if the defendant appears voluntarily (Schabas 2007: 257–258). Kenyan President Uhuru Kenyatta and the other Kenyan defendants, for instance, appeared voluntarily and were not arrested when the Prosecutor opened an investigation into the 2007 Kenyan election violence. When the Prosecutor makes a decision not to proceed with an investigation or prosecution, the Pre-Trial Chamber may review that decision at the request of the referring state or the Security Council, either of which may request that the Prosecutor reconsider it. The Pre-Trial Chamber may also review on its

© Springer International Publishing Switzerland 2015

A. Novak, *The International Criminal Court*, DOI 10.1007/978-3-319-15832-7_5

own initiative, in the "interests of justice," a decision of the Prosecutor not to proceed with a case (Kaul 2005: 378). Groome (2014: 6, 17–18) has identified several weaknesses in the Court's handling of early investigations, including issuance of indictments too soon in the investigation, overreliance on anonymous hearsay testimony, and the use of intermediaries, such as NGOs, to perform key investigative functions.

5.2 Arrest and Transfer of a Suspect to the Hague

Arrests for the Yugoslavia tribunal were often made by NATO troops or members of the Stabilization Force. In the current situations in Uganda or the Democratic Republic of the Congo, for instance, there are no such forces; planning an arrest requires cooperation between the states parties and the Prosecutor. The credibility of the Court could suffer if an arrest warrant issued by the Pre-Trial Chamber at the Prosecutor's request remained ineffective over a long period of time. The Court is located far from many of its investigations, with no police force of its own and no powers of enforcement. It is only as strong as the effective and ongoing cooperation by member states allows it to be (Kaul 2005: 383). All states parties are under an obligation to cooperate with the Court's requests. Where a state party fails to cooperate, the Court may refer the matter to the Assembly of States Parties, or, if the case arose from a UN Security Council referral, to the Security Council. The surrender to the Court of persons sought by it is indispensable to ICC proceedings. The Statute provides an unequivocal obligation to arrest and surrender a person sought by the Court; this is not discretionary for a state party, with only the marginal exception, discussed earlier, for agreements among states not to surrender each other's nationals under Article 93. Despite this legal obligation to comply, however, actual enforcement of these duties varies (Broomhall 2003: 155–159).

Most common law countries forbid trials *in absentia*. The accused, in other words, must be present for trial. By contrast, in civil law countries, where truth rather than procedural justice is the primary goal of a criminal trial, an *in absentia* proceeding may be permitted; such trials were allowed at Nuremberg. Whether to permit prosecution of a defendant who was not present for trial was a matter of significant debate before and during the Rome Conference, as opponents believed *in absentia* proceedings would be "show trials" that would make the Court appear ineffective, while proponents thought that the "moral sanction" of the proceedings could contribute to the isolation and capture of a defendant still at large. Because *in absentia* trials could violate due process, a state that extradites a prisoner to the Court based on an *in absentia* conviction could be in violation of its own obligations under international treaties (Shaw 2012: 113, 118–119, 124). In this, as in many other realms, the Rome Statute provides a negotiated compromise. Pre-Trial proceedings to confirm the charges against an accused may take place without the accused person's presence, but trial proceedings cannot be held *in absentia* unless a defendant has attempted to disrupt the proceeding. Furthermore an *in absentia* pre-trial hearing may only take place if a defendant has fled or cannot be found and the Court has taken all reasonable steps to inform the defendant of the charges and secure his or her presence (Trendafilova 2009: 451–452, 454).

5.3 Criminal Procedure

While the Yugoslavia and Rwanda tribunals were initially oriented toward the party-driven model of adversarial trials, typical of the common law tradition, under the Rome Statute judges play active roles in running the trial, as in an inquisitorial proceeding. Judges possess a large measure of influence and investigative autonomy during the trial, more than an adversarial system, though perhaps not as much as in a pure inquisitorial regime (Kaul 2005: 376). The procedural system laid down by the Rome Statute is unlike any domestic system; it is not adversarial or inquisitorial, nor is it strictly a hybrid of the two. Instead, it is a negotiated diplomatic compromise, possessing elements of other systems but also with unique procedural rules. Students of comparative criminal justice will recall that in an accusatorial or adversarial criminal justice proceeding, a judge makes decisions based only on evidence collected in oral form and in his presence in a public proceeding. By contrast, in an inquisitorial system, a judge's decisions are primarily based on evidence and written pleadings collected and assembled in a file or dossier during the investigation phase by a magistrate judge or procurator. The Rome Statute and the Rules of Evidence and Procedure generally provide that the parties themselves carry out questioning in the judge's presence and with a preference for live testimony. However, as in an inquisitorial system, statements gathered in the Pre-Trial phase may still be admitted or used at trial (Caianiello 2011: 392–393, 398). Caianiello (ibid.: 409) expresses concern that given the Prosecutor's dominant position in ICC proceedings, weakening the adversarial nature of the proceeding could place the defendant at a greater disadvantage.

The Pre-Trial and Trial proceedings at the Court are analytically distinct. The Pre-Trial Chamber tests whether the Prosecutor has made out a sufficient case to proceed, while the Trial Chamber decides the core issues of guilt and innocence. The Court's Rules of Procedure and Evidence allow for considerable maneuver room, and it is up to the judges to determine the boundaries of what is permitted. Critics have called the conceptual organization of the Court's criminal trial proceeding "confused," lacking a sense of direction and failing to truly unite the "best" elements of accusatorial and inquisitorial models (De Smet 2009: 407, 438). In making legal judgments, the Article 21 of the Rome Statute prioritizes the Statute itself and the Court's procedural rules in making a decision, but allows judges to consider treaties, applicable rules of international law, and general legal principles derived from different legal traditions or the countries where the crimes took place (Hochmayr 2014: 655–656).

5.3.1 Procedure at the Pre-Trial Chamber

The Pre-Trial phase is the preliminary phase of the criminal proceeding in which the case is investigated and prepared. At any time after initiating an investigation, the Prosecutor may seek a warrant of arrest, which will be confirmed by the Pre-Trial Chamber upon a showing of reasonable grounds that the person has committed a crime within the jurisdiction of the Court. Once a person has surrendered to the Court or has submitted to jurisdiction based on a summons, the Pre-Trial Chamber must subsequently confirm the charges. The Prosecutor must disclose to the defendant all of the evidence on which she intends to rely at the confirmation hearing, and the detained suspect may seek interim release (Nerlich 2012: 1340–1342). The judges of the Pre-Trial Chamber do not perform the duties of an "investigating judge" as in a civil law system; rather, the burden is squarely on the Prosecutor to gather evidence as in a common law system (De Smet 2009: 422). The Rome Statute permits the defense team to conduct an independent investigation, but encourages collaboration with the Prosecutor to ensure that efforts are not duplicative. However, the Court's legal aid scheme provides only limited funding for defense counsel to conduct investigations compared to the much larger resources of the Office of the Prosecutor (De Smet 2009: 424–425).

Although the judges of the Pre-Trial Chamber are tasked with "confirming" the charges of the indictment in order to act as a check on the Prosecutor against unsubstantiated accusations, the confirmation hearing is not a "mini-trial." At this stage, the Pre-Trial Chamber is scrutinizing the Prosecutor, not the accused. The Prosecutor does not need to prove charges beyond a reasonable doubt at this stage, only that there be "substantial grounds to believe" the charges, though the objective of ensuring that only properly substantiated trials proceed is in tension with avoiding duplication of the trial at the Pre-Trial stage (De Smet 2009: 428, 430; Nerlich 2012: 1347). Although the Court does not rely on a written dossier as in an inquisitorial proceeding, the record before the Pre-Trial Chamber is transmitted to the Trial Chamber for the organization of the case. This is to ensure public transparency. However, the Trial Chamber, as in a common law system, may only make decisions based on the evidence submitted and discussed at the trial—not on the Pre-Trial record (De Smet 2009: 434–435).

International criminal proceedings have special problems of disclosure. Generally speaking, the Prosecution is required to disclose to the defense the nature of the case and evidence against the defendant. In principle, the accused has an extensive right to disclosure of evidence, both inculpatory and exculpatory; in reality, the defense and prosecution engage in frequent battles over disclosure. Defense attorneys are entitled to timely release of evidence. However, the Prosecution is permitted to seek anonymity for witnesses at trial. At the *Lubanga* trial, the Prosecution relied on evidence received pursuant to a confidentiality agreement, which is permitted under the Rome Statute, and therefore was unable to reveal information about sources or witnesses. Another source of controversy was that because international tribunals lack police enforcement, prosecutors must often rely on unsavory witnesses or intermediaries simply because they are available. These concerns are magnified by the involvement of victims in the proceedings, who have their own legal representative. Thus, the defendant is facing two hostile opponents rather than one, which might increase the adversarial nature of proceedings. In the trial of Congolese defendant Germain Katanga, a frustrated defense complained that the Prosecutor was overly restrictive with materials disclosed to the defense and dumped a large amount of undifferentiated documents on the defense team (Morrissey 2012: 70–71, 84–92).

5.3.2 Procedure at the Trial Chamber

International war crimes trials are inherently messy. Milošević at the Yugoslavia tribunal, Charles Taylor at the Special Court for Sierra Leone, and Saddam Hussein at the Iraqi High Tribunal used self-representation to disrupt and delay the proceedings. Defendants often refuse to cooperate and may disrespect or interrupt the proceeding; in the worst cases, defendants can incite acts of violence while on the stand or resort to physical confrontation in the courtroom. Because of the political context and widespread publicity, leaders facing international prosecution are more likely than ordinary defendants to believe that they will not receive a fair trial (Scharf 2012: 25–26). Another common feature of international criminal proceedings is that they can be very lengthy, far lengthier than in most domestic systems. Reflecting both common and civil law traditions, criminal proceedings at the International Criminal Court have truth as their primary purpose rather than procedural justice, but the parties ultimately lead the trial presentation and the submission of evidence. Unlike common law judges, however, who are reliant on evidence submitted by the prosecution or defense team, judges of the Court's Trial Chamber have the power to "require" the production of evidence. The Trial Chamber may also modify the legal characterization of the facts, and legal analyses by the Pre-Trial Chamber do not bind the Trial Chamber (Nerlich 2012: 1350). The result of this procedure may be chaotic: the trial judges are more interventionist than a typical common law judge, but have less power over the proceedings than a typical civil law judge (De Smet 2009: 418–419).

5.4 The Role of the Registry

The Registry is responsible for the non-judicial aspects of the Court's administration. These include responsibilities related to witnesses, victims, defense, and public outreach. The Court's outreach activities have focused on countries where the Court has ongoing investigations in order to engage victims and local communities through NGOs and other local stakeholders in the Court's proceedings and to combat misinformation. The Registry also administers the reparations program and the Trust Fund for Victims in the event that a defendant is convicted, which are explored in the next chapter.

5.4.1 Witness Protection

The Rome Statute does not explicitly allow anonymous witness testimony, privileging instead the defendant's right to confront those accusing him or her. However, Article 68 of the Rome Statute requires that the Court take measures to protect the safety, physical and psychological well-being, and privacy of victims and witnesses who participate in the Court's proceedings. The provision also makes special reference in this regard to victims of gender-based and sexual violence. However, there is contrary precedent: the Yugoslavia tribunal did permit witnesses to testify anonymously after the *Tadić* judgment in 1995. In light of the fragile security situation in the Democratic Republic of the Congo, the ICC Trial Chamber followed suit in the Lubanga case in 2008, ruling that witnesses may testify anonymously so long as extreme care is taken not to prejudice a defendant's rights. The Rome Statute requires the Court to protect witnesses from retaliation or violence for testifying in a proceeding; certainly, doing otherwise would discourage other victims to come forward. At the same time, securing a conviction primarily based on testimony from a witness whom the defendant may not cross-examine surely would infringe a defendant's due process rights (Kurth 2009: 628, 631–632). In early 2015, the Court received word that a potential witness in the trial against Kenyan Vice President William Ruto had been abducted and murdered. In a press release, the Court indicated that the ICC Registry had offered him security measures, including a safe residency in a new location. According to the Court, a total of more than 650 witnesses, victims, and family members had received protective measures from the Court (International Criminal Court 2015).

5.4.2 Role of Victims

Unlike many domestic court systems and even the Yugoslav and Rwanda tribunals, the International Criminal Court makes provision for the informal involvement of victims in criminal proceedings beyond simply as testifying witnesses. Under the Rome Statute, victims must be informed if the Prosecutor or Pre-Trial Chamber decides not to proceed with an investigation. They are entitled to submit observations to the Court during proceedings and to take part in reparations hearings and appeals against reparation orders. However, they are not entitled to argue against the accused on appeal, and they have no right of appeal themselves. Although the Rome Statute does not specifically distinguish between victims who informally participate in criminal proceedings and victims who are specifically called to testify as witnesses, principles of due process require that witness testimony conform to the rules of evidence. For participating victims who are not called as witnesses, the ability to communicate their stories to the Court outside the formal rules of evidence could serve as a source of healing and help establish an overall narrative of the crime. It could also present its own due process challenges if the statements are given evidentiary weight (Haslam 2004: 322–327).

According to some observers, victims and others view participation as an element of restorative justice, seeing the truth-telling aspect of providing testimony and their contribution to the historical record as essential for personal and community restoration. The rules of evidence and procedure at the Court allow for a more open and free presentation of witness stories than would be possible in an adversarial system; this greater flexibility means that the development of the historical record at the trial has restorative potential beyond simply the creation of an evidentiary record by lawyers and interrogators. The Court's emphasis on witness testimony rather than documentary evidence by the ICC ensures that victims' stories have a greater impact in the trial outcomes. In addition, the potential for victims to provide evidence anonymously also indicates a shift away from the traditional adversarial criminal process (Findlay et al. 2013: 110–111). Inevitably, the Prosecutor's discretion to bring charges limits who may be recognized as a victim. For instance, by limiting the charges brought against Thomas Lubanga to the recruitment and use of child soldiers, the Prosecutor caused a rift with victims' representatives who believed that child soldiers represented only a small part of the alleged atrocities, including rape and sexual violence (Aptel 2012: 1367).

As of 2013, more than 12,000 individuals have applied to participate as victims in the proceedings before the International Criminal Court, with well over 5000 successfully obtaining victim status. According to SáCouto and Thompson (2014: 17), the process of applying for and approving victim status is inefficient and frustrating; they advocate a two-tiered approach in which witnesses wishing to appear at the tribunal must apply individually while all others may participate as a class with a common legal representative responsible for ensuring the eligibility of victims. Except for a handful of victims who were permitted to be present and testify in the earliest cases, today all victim participation in a proceeding takes place through a single lawyer, appointed by the Registry to represent the class of victims in a case. The lawyer attends status conferences and hearings, makes submissions, tenders evidence, examines witnesses, and delivers opening and closing statements on behalf of hundreds or thousands of victims (ibid.: 18–20). As Kendall and Nouwen (2013: 261–262) describe, this process may amalgamate victims into an abstract entity, "The Victims," while permitting only a very small number to actively participate in legal proceedings. In this way, the victim is simultaneously made to be both central and marginal to the proceeding (Clarke 2009: 237).

5.4.3 The Defense Bar

The quality of the defense bar strongly shapes the credibility of a criminal proceeding. Even at Nuremberg, some German defense lawyers were men of significant accomplishment, and one was even an academic in international law who contributed to the caliber of discussions—in sharp contrast to the corruption of the legal profession in Nazi Germany (Maley 2008: 7–8). To this end, the Rome Statute provides an enforceable right to defense counsel, although it stops short of clearly delineating the protections for defense counsel who wish to investigate in countries where evidence is located or the alleged crimes occurred. Instead, the negotiating parties in Rome deferred an agreement on protections for defense counsel, to be approved at a later date by the Assembly of States Parties (Gallant 2000: 22). The Rome Statute did not create a defense bar association, but envisioned one to be established later. Such an association would allow defense counsel to offer useful insights concerning proposed amendments to the rules, as the Rome Statute does not permit individuals to submit amendments themselves (Mundis 2003: 145). Today, organizations such as the International Criminal Defense Attorneys Organization in Montreal and the International Criminal Bar in The Hague help organize international criminal defense lawyers for advocacy and policy-making purposes at the ICC and other tribunals.

In general, the right to counsel under the Rome Statute is more protective than similar rights in the United States, the United Kingdom, and other domestic jurisdictions. Article 55 of the Rome Statute provides for the right to counsel at the earliest stages of a proceeding, even earlier than in many common law jurisdictions. When an individual is merely under suspicion of having committed a crime and before he or she is questioned, a defendant has the right to legal assistance of his or her choosing or appointed counsel if her she cannot afford a lawyer. An accused person has the right to remain silent and the right to be informed of grounds of prosecution before questioning takes place. Judges of the Pre-Trial Chamber may appoint counsel to represent the interests of future defendants, even where no person has yet been accused of a crime or an accused person is still at large. This may lead to later conflicts as counsel appointed so early in the proceeding may be representing multiple defendants whose rights are adverse to one another. However, as in civil law jurisdictions such as France or Germany, the judges of the Pre-Trial Chamber continue to closely supervise the Prosecutor during an investigation with an eye toward determining when to appoint individual counsel (Gallant 2000: 24). Even though a defendant's rights are protected, such as at Article 67 granting adequate time to prepare a defense and the right to be informed promptly of charges, defense counsel face a number of practical obstacles as a result of the unique nature of proceedings before the Court. Among these obstacles, as Khan and Shah (2013: 200) have observed, are late disclosure of evidence from the Prosecutor and the difficulties of learning the identities of witnesses and victims.

5.5 The Conviction

In order to convict, the Court must be convinced of guilt beyond a reasonable doubt, a notion familiar to the common law world. However, the civil law influence is evident in the Rome Statute's provisions allowing the Court to alter the legal characterization of the facts during or after the proceeding, finding an accused person guilty of one crime even if the initial indictment was for a different crime. The decision of the Trial Chamber must be reached by a majority vote of the three judges, although the Statute encourages unanimity. Judges must be present at all stages of the trial and during the deliberations; the President may also appoint an alternate fourth judge who can be present in order to replace a panel member who is unable to complete the case (Schabas 2007: 301–304). While proceedings against a defendant who dies during trial will be terminated, the Rome Statute and the Court's jurisprudence do not yet provide a clear procedure for the situation where a defendant dies after conviction but with pending appeals in his or her case (Bachvarova 2012: 548, 550).

In March 2012, the International Criminal Court issued its first verdict, finding Thomas Lubanga Dyilo of enlisting, conscripting, and using child soldiers in the Democratic Republic of the Congo. In 2012, the Court levied a sentence of fourteen years' imprisonment on Lubanga, with six years subtracted for time served, and a month later, the Court issued a decision outlining the procedure for awarding compensation and other reparations to victims. The Prosecution sought a 30-year sentence, but the Court failed to find aggravation as the charges that Lubanga ordered or encouraged the beatings of child soldiers were unproven. Reparations were made available to all victims, and not only the 85 who participated in the trial proceedings. The *Lubanga* decision set a jurisprudential model for decisions that were to come later (Amann 2012: 809–817). However, some observers expressed concern at the length of time between the close of a trial and the decision, the lack of clarity in the initial charges and the sentencing rationale, and the timing of the decision on reparations (SáCouto and Clearly 2014a, b). The *Lubanga* case and the others arising from the situation in the Democratic Republic of the Congo are explored further below.

5.6 Current Cases

Currently, there are nine situations pending before the International Criminal Court, all of which are on the continent of Africa. Two of these are in Central African Republic, and the other seven include Uganda, Democratic Republic of the Congo, Sudan (Darfur Province), Kenya, Libya, Côte d'Ivoire, and Mali. These have resulted in a total of 36 individuals to be involved in Court proceedings to this date, of whom nine are still at large, four are dead or likely dead, two have been convicted, one has been acquitted, one case was declared inadmissible, seven had had their charges dismissed or withdrawn, and two have been arrested or are in custody of national authorities and not yet transferred to the Court. The remaining defendants are currently still involved in proceedings.

Current situations before the International Criminal Court

Central African Republic	referred by government of Central African Republic	I: Crimes against humanity and war crimes for Congolese warlord operating in CAR	I: Jean-Pierre Bemba, trial is ongoing. Additional prosecutions against four others for witness tampering and falsifying evidence
		II: New investigation opened in September 2014 for crimes committed in civil war since 2012	II: No indictments issued yet in second referral; investigation ongoing
Uganda	referred by government of Uganda	Crimes against humanity and war crimes by Lord's Resistance Army campaign of terror in northern Uganda	Joseph Kony and three others still at large (one surrendered to authorities in January 2015)
Democratic Republic of the Congo	referred by government of DR Congo	Crimes against humanity and war crimes during Second Congo War, including Kivu and Ituri Provinces	Germain Katanga and Thomas Lubanga have been convicted; Lubanga is currently appealing sentence. Mathieu Chui was acquitted. One other case (Bosco Ntaganda) still in proceedings
Sudan	UN Security Council referral	Genocide, war crimes, and crimes against humanity in Darfur Province	None of the four current suspects are in custody; charges against another have been withdrawn; another has died
Kenya	*proprio motu* investigation by Prosecutor	Crimes against humanity in post-election violence orchestrated by politicians and paramilitaries	Case against Kenyan President Uhuru Kenyatta and former secretary to the Cabinet Francis Muthaura withdrawn for lack of evidence. Case against Vice President William Ruto may be withdrawn. Proceedings continue against radio station executive Joshua Sang, but two other cases were withdrawn or dismissed
Libya	UN Security Council referral	Crimes against humanity for crackdowns on protestors during Libya's Arab Spring revolt	Muammar Gaddafi has died, and case against Abdullah Senussi inadmissible pending trial in Libya. Saif Al-Islam Gaddafi arrested in Libya but not transferred to The Hague

(continued)

| Côte d'Ivoire | *proprio motu* investigation by Prosecutor | Crimes against humanity in Ivorian civil war when former President Laurent Gbagbo lost reelection but refused to leave office | Gbagbo and associate Charles Blé Gardé in Pre-Trial phase. Gbagbo's wife Simone arrested but facing trial in Côte d'Ivoire |
| Mali | referred by government of Mali | War crimes and crimes against humanity committed during civil war between Tuareg rebels and government | No indictments have been issued; investigation ongoing |

5.6.1 Democratic Republic of the Congo

The conflict in the eastern region of the Democratic Republic of the Congo has been among the most destructive in the world in the past two decades. Atrocities continued in Ituri Province after July 1, 2002, when the Rome Statute entered into force, and with it, jurisdiction over the Democratic Republic of the Congo, already a state party. In 2003, the Prosecutor Luis Moreno Ocampo announced that he had selected the situation in Ituri as the most urgent situation for investigation, and the following year President Joseph Kabila referred the situation in his country to the Court for all crimes occurring after July 1, 2002. On June 21, 2004, the Prosecutor announced that he found reasonable basis to commence an investigation, and in October, the Congolese government signed an agreement with the Court to protect investigators and turn over government documents (Arsanjani and Reisman 2005: 398). The Congolese investigation suffered procedural setbacks, however, when ICC staff received a large amount of material from UN officials in the Congo on the understanding that the evidence would not be used at trial. Because of these confidentiality arrangements, the Prosecutor refused to turn over evidence to judges or defense lawyers and, at one point, faced dismissal of the case until the UN waived confidentiality of many documents. The episode may affect the willingness of the UN or other parties to give the Court confidential or sensitive information in the future (Bosco 2014: 138–140).

The situation in the Democratic Republic of the Congo presents special challenges, as the multiparty conflict is ongoing, with allegations of abuses by all sides. The conflicts in Kivu and Ituri provinces sparked intervention from foreign powers such as Rwanda and Uganda. In addition, the Congo's own violence has spilled over into Chad, the Central African Republic, South Sudan, and northern Uganda. The Prosecutor had difficulty conducting any meaningful investigation on the ground and reaching the accused persons as a result of the state of insecurity and the prevalence of landmines. The Congolese government has promised assistance, but the government's ineffective rule over the territory was one of the reasons for its initial referral (Arsanjani and Reisman 2005: 398). Human rights groups and victim communities have criticized the Prosecutor's strategy as selective and partial in favor of ruling elites within the government and military. All of the indicted individuals are political opponents of President Kabila and his government's authority in the eastern region. One of them even subsequently became an ally of President Kabila after the indictments were issued and he was shielded from arrest, but Kabila turned him over to the Court when he defected (Tiemessen 2014: 452).

As explained above, the convictions of Thomas Lubanga and Germain Katanga were the first two issued by the International Criminal Court. The Court's decision in *Lubanga* rigorously analyzed the child soldiers issue, but the Prosecutor's decision not to prosecute crimes of sexual violence in addition to the recruitment of child soldiers and the failure to disclose exculpatory evidence to the defense, twice causing the suspension of proceedings, were more controversial (Amman 2012: 810; Wiersing 2012: 22). One of Lubanga's paramilitary rivals, Mathieu Ngudjolo Chui, was prosecuted for the February 2003 assault on the village of Bogoro, which had been under Lubanga's control. As many as 200 people died in the attack, almost all unarmed civilians. Chui was acquitted by the International Criminal Court in 2012, upheld on appeal in 2015, but Germain Katanga, who also participated in the Bogoro attack, was convicted and sentenced to twelve years' imprisonment in March 2014 (Bosco 2014: 140–141). Katanga's conviction, however, provoked a dissent from one of the judges because the Prosecutor altered the charges against him after the trial opened. Bosco Ntaganda, a powerful militia commander in the eastern Congo, turned himself into the Court in March 2013 and is now involved in proceedings. One defendant, Sylvestre Mudacumara, remains at large (Tiemessen 2014: 452).

5.6.2 Northern Uganda

On December 16, 2003, Uganda referred the situation concerning the Lord's Resistance Army (LRA) to the Prosecutor, the first time that a state party had voluntarily submitted a case. Uganda was motivated by a desire to "internationalize" a conflict that had reached a stalemate and that attracted little attention from powerful states, leaving Uganda alone to negotiate a peaceful settlement with a ruthless, cult-like guerrilla force. The LRA referral raised the question of whether a state with a functioning judicial system—both willing and able to prosecute—could voluntarily relinquish jurisdiction in favor of the International Criminal Court. The referral has been successful in changing the situation on the ground, especially by placing international pressure on Sudan to end support for the LRA in an effort to destabilize now-independent South Sudan, which in turn increased the LRA's political isolation (Akhavan 2005: 403–404).

The conflict in Northern Uganda has partial roots in colonial divisions that favored the southern, largely Bantu ethnic groups and treated the northern Nilotic groups as laborers and soldiers. Uganda's former presidents Milton Obote and Idi

Amin were both northerners with a military background, but Yoweri Museveni, who led the National Resistance Army to power in 1986, forced the Acholi people to retreat to the north. His army perpetuated revenge killings and massacres and engendered many northerners, especially Acholi, to join new rebel groups. Led by a young female spirit medium named Alice Lakwena, a religiopolitical guerrilla force named the Holy Spirit Movement rapidly advanced to the capital city, but was eventually defeated by the Ugandan military and reorganized by Joseph Kony—said to have inherited Alice's spirit—as the LRA. The Acholi, tired of war, became targets of the brutal tactics used by the LRA, which stockpiled weapons, trained soldiers, and raided northern Uganda from bases in what is now South Sudan (Baines 2007: 98–100).

After sustained lobbying by Acholi elders, civil society, and religious leaders, the government of Uganda passed the Amnesty Act in 2000, granting individual combatants of the Lord's Resistance Army and other paramilitary groups immunity from prosecution. In 2004, the International Criminal Court's indictments challenged the validity of the Amnesty Act and triggered the long-running "peace versus justice" debate about whether amnesty paved the way for an end to the conflict or granted impunity for atrocities (Anyeko et al. 2012: 108–109). The Acholi are one of the first victim populations to lobby their government for a blanket amnesty. The government only reluctantly passed the amnesty, intending it to facilitate the return of rebels. According to the amnesty, if the rebels pledged to denounce the rebellion, they would be protected from formal prosecution, given reintegration packages, and resettled into camps. Local leaders believed that the International Criminal Court's indictments would undermine the amnesty and efforts to initiate peace talks. Given the traditional emphasis on reconciliation, communal accountability, and forgiveness in Acholi culture, local and religious leaders believed the amnesty law better incorporated these elements than international prosecution. The ICC Prosecutor attempted to accommodate local demands and withheld releasing indictments of the LRA until October 2005 to allow a new but ultimately unsuccessful peace negotiation to take place. The chief mediator, Ugandan government minister and ethnic Acholi Betty Bigombe, expressed her frustrations with Moreno Ocampo's decision to prosecute. The ICC continues to be perceived as an obstacle to peace: Kony and other high-level leaders have repeatedly threatened to end talks should the ICC Prosecutor pursue the indictments (Baines 2007: 101–102). In 2006, Kony met with a senior UN official and stated that he wanted the ICC warrants lifted as a condition for entering into formal peace talks, though negotiations eventually collapsed in 2008. The Court was placed in an awkward position as an obstacle to a peace process (Bosco 2014: 129–131). By 2011, about 24,000 individuals had reported to authorities, renounced involvement in the war, and surrendered weapons in their positions in return for amnesty (McNamara 2013: 660).

Currently, Kony and three others wanted by the Court are still at large, while one defendant has died. In January 2015, news reports indicated that Dominic Ongwen had surrendered to American forces stationed in the Central African

Republic (BBC News 2015). Uganda has also begun domestic prosecutions of LRA commanders. In 2008, Uganda established the International Crimes Division (ICD) of the High Court to try individuals for war crimes. In 2011, the ICD heard its first case against Thomas Kwoyelo, for 53 charges of war crimes, though Kwoyelo eventually received amnesty under the Amnesty Act of 2000 and was ordered release by the Constitutional Court. However, his case was appealed to the Ugandan Supreme Court, and the decision may affect the legality of all amnesties issued under the Amnesty Act if the Supreme Court determines that an amnesty for war crimes is unlawful (McNamara 2013: 666, 671).

5.6.3 Sudan (Darfur Province)

The Darfur conflict was rooted in historically complicated relationships between Arab and non-Arab (African) tribes. The Arab government in Khartoum has gradually disenfranchised the non-Arab peoples in Sudan, despite similarities in language and religion. Rebel groups acting against the Khartoum government, including the Sudan Liberation Army and the Justice Equality Movement, sought greater political representation. The President of Sudan, Omar al-Bashir, who came to power in 1989, has long sought to quell the Darfur-based rebel movements, providing Arab *Janjaweed* militiamen with military supplies. The *Janjaweed* uprooted about one million people in the Darfur region, however, and the atrocities perpetuated by the militia force bear hallmarks of ethnic or racial targeting that may fit the definition of genocide. The United States government announced in September 2004 that genocide was occurring, though a UN-backed panel found only crimes against humanity and war crimes rather than genocide (Falligant 2010: 735–738).

In March 2005, the United Nations Security Council referred the situation in Darfur to the Office of the Prosecutor, and an investigation was opened June 1, 2005. As then-Prosecutor Moreno Ocampo writes, the Office of the Prosecutor spent twenty months reviewing thousands of documents and interviewing victims. In April 2007, the Pre-Trial Chamber issued arrest warrants against Ahmad Harun, former minister of the interior and humanitarian affairs, and Ali Kushayb, a *Janjaweed* militia leader, for war crimes and crimes against humanity. The Prosecutor showed that they joined together to attack civilians in Darfur by coordinating a system in which the *Janjaweed* militia supplemented the Sudanese army and incited it to attack the civilian population. In December 2007, Moreno Ocampo informed the Security Council that Sudan was not cooperating with the Court. In Darfur, Ahmad Harun's plan was to force people out of villages and into camps—camps that he tightly controlled. Finally, on July 14, 2008, Moreno Ocampo requested an arrest warrant against Sudanese President Omar al-Bashir for three counts of genocide, five of crimes against humanity, and two of war crimes (Moreno Ocampo 2011: 285).

Sudanese President Omar Al-Bashir, indicted by the International Criminal Court for genocide, war crimes, and crimes against humanity in Darfur Province. *By U.S. Navy photo by Mass
Communication Specialist 2nd Class Jesse B. Awalt/Released (DefenseImagery.mil, VIRIN
090131-N-0506A-342) [Public domain],* **via** *Wikimedia Commons*

Al-Bashir is currently the only defendant at the International Criminal Court
indicted on charges of genocide. As Prunier (2011: 46–48) explains, the definition of genocide under the Genocide Convention was almost entirely driven by a
specific historical event, the 1941–1945 genocide of the European populations of
Jewish origin by the Nazi Party of Germany. The Darfur genocide does not precisely fit the "Holocaust paradigm," because the ethnicities of the victims and the
perpetrators are not overwhelmingly distinct from one another; the persecuted
groups managed to fight back to some degree with their own militias; and the
worst agents of the violence were *Janjaweed* militiamen who were not necessarily
acting on behalf of the Government of Sudan, though they may have been acting
with its knowledge and implicit consent.

Despite the promise of a Security Council referral, the International Criminal
Court has not received cooperation from member states to arrest al-Bashir.
Prosecutor Moreno Ocampo condemned countries that allowed al-Bashir to travel
in international airspace, pointedly including meetings of the Arab League and
the African Union, and even including travels to countries that were states parties to the Rome Statute. The indictments against the President of Sudan elicited
an African backlash that Moreno Ocampo had overreached, and Western powers (including Security Council members) failed to place significant pressure on
Sudan to turn al-Bashir over to the Court (Bosco 2014: 155–159). In 2010, Chad

and Kenya, both states parties to the Rome Statute, each hosted al-Bashir at official functions and explained to the Assembly of State Parties that he had immunity from arrest. In October 2010, the Pre-Trial Chamber requested that Kenya
report any problems that would impede or prevent al-Bashir's arrest and surrender
when he visited the country (van der Vyver 2011: 684–686). The Rome Statute's
provisions on sovereign immunity have been subject to considerable debate.
Although al-Bashir does not have sovereign immunity from prosecution before
the International Criminal Court under Article 27 of the Rome Statute, the Court
still must gain physical custody of him as it cannot try him *in absentia*; for this,
it needs a state to make the arrest. Article 27 only abrogates sovereign immunity
before the Court itself; al-Bashir may still have sovereign immunity while he is in
the territory of other countries. Thus, though he can be prosecuted, it is possible
that he cannot be arrested (Needham 2011: 220). This gray area has worked to
al-Bashir's advantage. He remains in power in Sudan, if diplomatically isolated,
and none of the other Sudanese defendants have been apprehended. In December
2014, Prosecutor Bensouda announced that she was suspending the Sudan investigation in order to shift resources to other more urgent situations as a result of
the stalemate and an apparent lack of interest by the UN Security Council (BBC
News 2014b).

5.6.4 *Central African Republic*

Central African Republic has been a source of political instability since independence from France in 1960, most recently with the 2003 overthrow of President
Ange-Félix Patassé by chief of staff François Bozizé. In order to contain
Bozizé's forces as they marched on Bangui, the capital, Patassé requested support from Congolese warlord Jean-Pierre Bemba, who successfully held Bozizé's
forces back for five months while committing serious atrocities. After Bozizé
finally took power, the Central African Republic referred the country's situation
to the International Criminal Court in 2004 (Vinck and Pham 2010: 426). The
Prosecutor opened an investigation into crimes committed in that country since
2002, including the killing and rape of civilians by Bemba and the Movement for
the Liberation of the Congo. The Prosecutor issued an arrest warrant for Bemba
in 2008. Bemba, a former Vice President of the Democratic Republic of Congo,
was arrested during a visit to Belgium on charges of war crimes and crimes
against humanity (Stewart 2014: 149–50). The ICC released the arrest warrant
for Bemba only after he had lost the 2006 national elections in the Democratic
Republic of the Congo where he ran for president against Kabila, winning more
than 40 % of the vote. This evidenced further caution by the Prosecutor's office,
and his swift arrest in Belgium was state cooperation with the ICC at its best
(Bosco 2014: 141). During the Bemba trial, four individuals were arrested on
charges of corruptly influencing witnesses during proceedings, including brib-
ery and falsification of documents. Those arrested were Bemba's lead counsel,

a member of his defense team, a defense witness, and a Congolese Member of Parliament. This was the first instance of the Court prosecuting "secondary" crimes related to the conduct of its proceedings, which are prohibited by Article 70 of the Rome Statute. These trials remain pending, as does one for an individual involved in witness tampering in the Kenyan investigation (International Justice Resource Center 2013).

In 2007, the ICC established a field office in Bangui, Central African Republic, to increase awareness and general understanding among the general public of the Court's role and to ensure that local media outlets are given rapid and accurate information on legal developments. The outreach by the field office includes the radio series "Understanding the ICC," broadcasted in the Sango language, and "Ask the Court," broadcasted in French (Vinck and Pham 2010: 427). In March 2013, President Bozizé was overthrown by the largely Muslim Séléka rebel forces. In September 2014, the Court opened a second investigation into war crimes and crimes against humanity in Central African Republic, including murder, rape, and the use of child soldiers, by the Séléka and by a largely Christian anti-Bozizé militia. Human rights groups say thousands of civilians have been killed and a quarter of the population internally displaced. The conflict continues, and peacekeeping forces from the UN, the African Union, and France have been deployed (Steinhauser, September 24, 2014).

5.6.5 Kenya

On March 31, 2010, the Prosecutor issued a decision authorizing the first *proprio motu* investigation into the violence following Kenya's elections in 2007. After the presidential election results on December 27, 2007, ethnically-driven political violence led to about 1200 people killed, 3500 injured, and over 350,000 displaced. Under pressure from the African Union and UN Secretary-General Kofi Annan, both President Mwai Kibaki's Party of National Unity and opponent Raila Odinga's Orange Democratic Movement agreed to a power-sharing government. The coalition government subsequently established an independent commission of inquiry (the Waki Commission) that recommended a hybrid special tribunal in which Kenya could prosecute the architects of the violence, or, in the alternative, that Annan was to forward a confidential list of suspects to the ICC Prosecutor for possible investigation. Kenyan lawmakers twice rejected establishing a special tribunal, and Annan consequently transmitted the list of suspects to The Hague. Prosecutor Moreno Ocampo requested authorization from the Pre-Trial Chamber to investigate, and by a 2 to 1 vote, the Pre-Trial Chamber agreed (Jalloh 2011: 541–542; Brighton 2012: 642). The Prosecutor issued summonses for six people on the basis of crimes against humanity: then-Deputy Prime Minister Uhuru Kenyatta, then-Ministers Henry Kosgey and William Ruto, then-Cabinet Secretary Francis Muthaura, radio executive Joshua Arap Sang, and former police commissioner Mohammed Hussein Ali.

President Uhuru Kenyatta of Kenya, indicted by the International Criminal Court for crimes against humanity after Kenya's election-related violence in 2007. *By Nairobi123 (State House of Kenya/Government of Kenya) [public domain]*, **via** *Wikimedia Commons*

The dissenting judge in the Pre-Trial Chamber would have denied the Prosecutor's *proprio motu* investigation because he believed it fell short of the elements required for a crime against humanity—in particular, the Kenyan election violence was not organized or directed pursuant to a high-level state or organizational policy. The majority found, however, that the ethnic-based violence was organized by local leaders, businessmen, and politicians affiliated with the two major political parties, and therefore was conducted pursuant to an organizational policy. Certainly, the Rome Statute would not permit prosecution of a "crime against humanity" when committed by a wholly private actor; the pertinent question was whether violence orchestrated by political parties constituted an official or quasi-governmental policy. The Pre-Trial Chamber's decision, confirmed by the Appeals Chamber in a 4 to 1 vote in August 2011, may broaden the definition of "crime against humanity" (Jalloh 2011: 546–547). In addition, on appeal Kenya argued that the ICC should suspend prosecutions until Kenya has the opportunity to prosecute all of the suspects in the election violence, including the "Ocampo Six" as the indicted officials were known in the Kenyan press. Neither the Pre-Trial Chamber nor the Appeals Chamber accepted that Kenya was genuinely willing to take concrete steps to investigate the six suspects. Nonetheless, in March 2013 Kenyatta was elected President of Kenya and Ruto Vice President (Jalloh 2012: 121–22; Brighton 2012: 645–647, 658). Mueller (2014: 38) writes that the defendants used delay to postpone their trials until after they gained power.

On December 5, 2014, the Prosecutor withdrew charges of crimes against humanity against President Kenyatta after repeated requests to the Pre-Trial Chamber for extensions of time. According to the Prosecutor, the Kenyan government refused to hand over vital evidence and witnesses had been bribed and intimidated; consequently, the Prosecutor would not be able to prove Kenyatta's criminal responsibility beyond a reasonable doubt (BBC News 2014a). The case is a cautionary tale of the Court's weakness when it lacks state cooperation in an investigation. Although the cases against Ruto and Sang are still pending, they too face investigatory and evidentiary challenges. In 1999, Kenya became an early ratifier of the Rome Statute largely due to pressure from human rights groups; at the time, it seemed inconceivable that any Kenyan would ever be charged by the ICC. However, as Kenya's political risk increased, so too did the government's hostility toward the tribunal (Mueller 2014: 29, 37).

5.6.6 Libya

The Libyan conflict and investigation moved much more rapidly than other prosecutions. Inspired by events in Tunisia and Egypt, the people of Eastern Libya began an uprising against the government of Muammar Gaddafi in February 2011 and took control of several towns, including Benghazi, Libya's second-largest city. However, Gaddafi's use of lethal and indiscriminate violence on unarmed protesters enraged the international community. On February 26, 2011, the Security Council unanimously approved a referral for Libya, though, as in Darfur, it refused to provide funds to the Court from the UN budget. An international coalition commenced an air and missile campaign against Libyan government forces, and the North Atlantic Treaty Organization (NATO) intervened on the side of the rebels on March 27, 2011. Gaddafi was killed in fighting in October 2011, which effectively brought about the end of the conflict (Apuuli 2012: 138–140). As President, Gaddafi was an outspoken critic of the International Criminal Court, and he strenuously condemned the arrest warrant for al-Bashir. Gaddafi's relative isolation, the defection of senior Libyan diplomats, and the Arab League's condemnation of the state-sanctioned violence unleashed by his regime on protestors produced an unusual dynamic in which Russia, China, and the United States were willing to accept a referral (Bosco 2014: 166–172).

In May 2011, the Office of the Prosecutor filed an application with the Pre-Trial Chamber seeking warrants against Muammar Gaddafi, his son Saif Al-Islam Gaddafi, and his brother-in-law and intelligence chief Abdullah Al-Senussi for crimes against humanity. The unusual speed with which the Prosecutor Luis Moreno Ocampo moved in Libya was reminiscent of the ICTY's speed in acting against Milošević in 1999 after the Kosovo conflict broke out. Moreno Ocampo's investigation found that the Gaddafi regime engaged in systematic arrest, torture, rape, killing, deportation, and enforced disappearances of civilians suspected of supporting the uprising; used imprecise weaponry in crowded urban areas; deliberately targeted medical facilities; blocked humanitarian supplies; used civilians as human shields; enlisted child soldiers; and mistreated journalists (Ierace 2012: 106–110). Because Gaddafi was killed in the violence, proceedings against him were terminated shortly after. The Pre-Trial Chamber declared the case against Abdullah Al-Senussi inadmissible because proceedings were then being brought against him in Libya, which triggered the complementarity provisions, a decision upheld by the Appeals Chamber. Saif Al-Islam Gaddafi was arrested in Libya, but has not been turned over to the Court pending trial in Libya. He continues to face two counts of crimes against humanity before the ICC. The case poses a challenge for the doctrine of complementarity: although Libya wishes to prosecute him, some observers believe that he risks a sham trial and a quick execution unless he is transferred to The Hague (Bishop 2013: 420).

5.6.7 Côte D'Ivoire

Côte d'Ivoire originally accepted the Court's ad hoc jurisdiction in 2003 and subsequently ratified the Rome Statute in 2013. The current situation began on October 31, 2010, when the country held a long-delayed presidential election as a step toward ending the civil war that began in September 2002. Because neither President Laurent Gbagbo nor his main competitor Alassane Ouattara received a majority of the vote, a second round election was held on November 28, 2010. Ouattara won the election, but Gbagbo refused to accept the results and did not vacate office, attempting to manipulate the Constitutional Council into deeming the elections invalid and directing a campaign of terror against Ouattara supporters. After several months of clashes, Ouattara launched a successful military offensive that led to Gbagbo's arrest (Apuuli 2012: 137–138). About 3000 people died in the post-election violence in Côte d'Ivoire. In 2011, the Prosecutor opened a *proprio motu* investigation for crimes committed after November 2010, but subsequently expanded the scope to include events since September 2002. In 2012, an arrest warrant was issued for former President Gbagbo, for crimes against humanity that occurred in post-election violence, and his wife Simone (Stewart 2014: 152–153). In June 2014, the Pre-Trial Chamber confirmed the charges against Laurent Gbagbo, and scheduled a trial before the Trial Chamber. In September 2014, Pre-Trial Chamber confirmed charges against Gbagbo's associate Charles Blé Goudé, who led a youth movement. However, Côte d'Ivoire has declined to send Simone Gbagbo to The Hague, instead putting her on trial before a domestic court. On December 11, 2014, the Court's Pre-Trial Chamber ruled that her case was still admissible, as the charges she faced in Côte d'Ivoire were not the same as those brought by the Office of the Prosecutor. The case will be yet another test of the principle of complementarity: The Court has not yet investigated any party on the side of President Ouattara, though forces under his command are alleged to have committed abuses as well (Human Rights Watch 2014; BBC News 2014c).

5.6.8 Mali

The Court's most recent investigation concerns alleged war crimes and crimes against humanity committed in northern Mali since January 2012. Northern Mali was a site of contested control between the government and Tuareg rebel forces, who briefly declared an independent state of Azawad in 2012. French intervention allowed the government to reclaim most of the region, and a peace deal effectively ended the conflict in June 2013, though fighting resumed in September 2013. No arrest warrants have been issued in the Mali situation, and the case is still under investigation. These crimes included the murders of up to 150 Malian soldiers and 16 unarmed Muslim preachers, amputations, conscription and use of child soldiers, extrajudicial executions, attacks on cultural and religious sites, pillage of large cities, and more than 50 cases of rape. The Government of Mali referred the situation in July 2012. Unlike Côte d'Ivoire, Mali was already a state party to the Rome Statute (Stewart 2014: 153; Stegmiller 2013: 491–492).

5.6.9 Other Situations of Interest

The Court has investigated a number of other situations worldwide, but without bringing charges. These situations have included Afghanistan, Colombia, Iraq, Palestine, Georgia, Guinea, Honduras, and Ukraine, though the investigations of these situations are in various stages and several are in limbo. Fatou Bensouda, who took office as Prosecutor in 2012, has continued the cautious strategy of her predecessor, Luis Moreno Ocampo. The Court has remained quiet on the Russia-Georgia conflict in 2008 and on Afghanistan, perhaps because of the involvement of major powers in those conflicts. The Prosecutor's office continued monitoring Colombia (Bosco 2014: 174–175). As noted in the previous chapter, the Court will have to determine whether the Colombia situation is admissible based on the principle of complementarity, as Colombia has made some legal efforts to prosecute those responsible in crimes against humanity and war crimes during the long-running civil war with paramilitary groups and organized crime syndicates. Afghanistan is a major omission, as it is a state party to the ICC and undoubtedly the site of serious mass atrocities, including as many as 20,000 civilians killed since 2001. It has been stuck in the preliminary investigation phase for six years, possibly because of the Prosecutor's reluctance to raise the ire of the United States and other major powers that are heavily invested in the country. On December 2, 2014, the Office of the Prosecutor released the Report on Preliminary Examination Activities for 2014. The report details a number of mass atrocities that have been perpetrated by the Taliban, including civilian attacks, conscription of children for use as suicide bombers, and sexual and gender-based violence against girls and women. The report also scrutinizes pro-government forces, including the U.S. military, for mistreatment and torture of detainees and prisoners, and acknowledges that these charges could form the basis of another case (Office of the Prosecutor 2014). Preliminary investigations of non-parties cannot take place without a Security Council referral; candidates for a referral include North Korea, where the use of torture and forced labor camps has been documented, and Syria, where chemical weapons were used during the current civil war. The Islamic State's targeted persecution of the Yazidi minority in northern Iraq could also be the basis for a future Security Council referral.

5.7 Discussion Questions

1. Do you think the drafters of the Rome Statute intended a country like Uganda, willing and able to prosecute the Lord's Resistance Army, to refer cases to the Court? What are the risks involved?
2. Which international situations can you think of that should be before the International Criminal Court but are not yet being investigated or prosecuted?

5.8 Further Reading

For additional reading on the Ugandan situation, Tim Allen's book *Trial Justice: The International Criminal Court and the Lord's Resistance Army* (Zed Books 2006) takes a broad view of the conflict. Sosteness Francis Materu provides in-depth background and analysis of the Kenyan situation in his book, *The Post-Election Violence in Kenya*: Domestic and International Legal Responses (Springer 2014). Students interested in the trial procedures of the International Criminal Court may find helpful Karin N. Calvo-Goller's *The Trial Proceedings of the International Criminal Court: ICTY and ICTR Precedents* (Martinus Nijhoff 2006). In addition, students may be interested in the academic journals *International Criminal Law Review* (Brill) and *Journal of International Criminal Justice* (Oxford University Press), both of which extensively publish on recent scholarship on the International Criminal Court's current practice and procedure.

References

Akhavan, P. (2005). The Lord's Resistance Army case: Uganda's submission of the first state referral to the International Criminal Court. *American Journal of International Law*, 403–421.

Amman, D. M. (2012). *Prosecutor v. Lubanga. American Journal of International Law, 106*, 809–817.

Anyeko, K., Baines, E., Komakech, E., Ojok, B., Ogora, L. O., & Victor, L. (2012). "The cooling of hearts": Community truth-telling in Northern Uganda. *Human Rights Review, 13*, 107–124.

Aptel, C. (2012). Prosecutorial discretion at the ICC and victims' right to remedy: Narrowing the impunity gap. *Journal of International Criminal Justice, 10*, 1357–1375.

Apuuli, K. P. (2012). The African Union's notion of African solutions to African problems' and the crises in Côte d'Ivoire (2010-2011) and Libya (2011). *African Journal on Conflict Resolution, 12*, 135–160.

Arsanjani, M. H., & Reisman, W. M. (2005). The law-in-action of the International Criminal Court. *American Journal of International Law, 99*, 385–403.

Bachvarova, T. (2012). Impact of the death of a convicted person on pending proceedings before the International Criminal Court. *Journal of International Criminal Justice, 10*, 547–559.

Baines, E. K. (2007). The haunting of Alice: Local approaches to justice and reconciliation in Northern Uganda. *The International Journal of Transitional Justice, 1*, 91–114.

BBC News. (2014a, December 5). *ICC drops Uhuru Kenyatta charges for Kenya election violence.* Available at: http://www.bbc.com/news/world-africa-30347019.

BBC News. (2014b, December 12). *ICC prosecutor shelves Darfur War crimes inquiries.* Available at: http://www.bbc.com/news/world-africa-30458347.

BBC News. (2014c, December 26). *Ivory Coast trial of Simone Gbagbo begins.* Available at: http://www.bbc.com/news/world-africa-30604755.

BBC News. (2015, January 7). *LRA Rebel Dominic Ongwen surrenders to US forces in CAR.* Available at: http://www.bbc.com/news/world-africa-30705649.

Bishop, A. (2013). Failure of complementarity: The future of the International Criminal Court following the Libyan admissibility challenge. *Minnesota Journal of International Law, 22,* 388–421.

Bosco, D. (2014). *Rough justice: The International Criminal Court in a world of power politics.* New York: Oxford University Press.

Brighton, C. (2012). Avoiding unwillingness: Addressing the political pitfalls inherent in the complementarity regime of the International Criminal Court. *International Criminal Law Review, 12,* 629–664.

Broomhall, B. (2003). *International justice and the International Criminal Court: Between sovereignty and the rule of law.* New York: Oxford University Press.

Caianiello, M. (2011). First decisions on the admission of evidence at ICC trials: A blending of accusatorial and inquisitorial models? *Journal of International Criminal Justice, 9,* 385–410.

Clarke, K. M. (2009). *Fictions of justice: The International Criminal Court and the challenge of legal pluralism in Sub-Saharan Africa.* New York: Cambridge University Press.

De Smet, S. (2009). A structural analysis of the role of the pre-trial chamber in the fact-finding process of the ICC. In C. Stahn & G. Sluiter (Eds.), *The emerging practice of the International Criminal Court* (pp. 405–440). Boston: Martinus Nijhoff Publishers.

Falligant, J. (2010). The prosecution of Sudanese President Al Bashir: Why a Security Council deferral would harm the legitimacy of the International Criminal Court. *Wisconsin International Law Journal, 27,* 727–756.

Findlay, M., Kuo, L. B., & Wei, L. S. (2013). *International and comparative criminal justice: A critical introduction.* New York: Routledge.

Gallant, K. S. (2000). The role and powers of defense counsel in the Rome Statute of the International Criminal Court. *International Lawyer, 34,* 21–44.

Groome, D. (2014). No witnesses, no case: An assessment of the conduct and quality of ICC investigations. *Penn State Journal of Law and International Affairs, 3,* 1–29.

Haslam, E. (2004). Victim participation at the International Criminal Court: A triumph of hope over experience? In D. McGoldrick, P. Rowe & E. Donnelly (Eds.), *The permanent International Criminal Court: Legal and policy issues* (pp. 315–334). Portland, OR: Hart Publishing.

Hochmayr, G. (2014). Applicable law in practice and theory: Interpreting Article 21 of the ICC statute. *Journal of International Criminal Justice 12*:655–679.

Human Rights Watch. (2014, December 11). *Côte d'Ivoire: Surrender Simone Gbagbo to the ICC.* Available at: http://www.hrw.org/news/2014/12/11/cote-d-ivoire-surrender-simone-gbagbo-icc.

Ierace, M. (2012). Complexities in prosecuting international crimes: The ICC Libyan warrants. In G. Boas, W. A. Schabas & M. P. Scharf (Eds.) *International criminal justice: Legitimacy and coherence* (pp. 105–122). Northampton, MA: Edward Elgar.

International Criminal Court. (2015, January 6). Press release: ICC deeply concerned with *reported death of Mr. Meshack Yebei; stands ready to assist Kenyan investigations.* ICC-CPI-20150106-PR1081. Available at: www.icc-cpi.int.

International Justice Resource Center. (2013, December 3). *Four arrested for witness tampering in International Criminal Court trial of Jean-Pierre Bemba.* Available at: http://www.ijrcenter.org/2013/12/03/four-arrested-for-witness-tampering-in-trial-of-jean-pierre-bemba-gombo-at-the-international-criminal-court.

Jalloh, C. C. (2011). International decisions: Situation in the Republic of Kenya. *American Journal of International Law, 105*(3), 540–547.

Jalloh, C. C. (2012). International decisions: Situation in the Republic of Kenya. *American Journal of International Law, 106*, 118–125.

Kaul, H.-P. (2005). Construction site for more justice: The International Criminal Court after two years. *American Journal of International Law 99*, 370–384.

Kendall, S., & Sarah, N. (2013). Representational practices at the International Criminal Court: The gap between juridified and abstract victimhood. *Law and Contemporary Problems 76*, 235–262.

Khan, K. A. A. & Shah, A. A. . 2013. Defensive practices: Representing clients before the International Criminal Court. *Law and Contemporary Problems, 76*, 191–233.

Kurth, M. E. (2009). Anonymous witness before the International Criminal Court: Due process in dire straits. In C. Stahn & G. Sluiter (Eds.), *The emerging practice of the International Criminal Court* (pp. 615–634). Boston: Martinus Nijhoff Publishers.

Maley, W. (2008). The atmospherics of the nuremberg trial. In D. A. Blumenthal & T. L. H. McCormack (Eds.), *The legacy of nuremberg: Civilising influence or institutionalised vengeance?* (pp. 3–12). Boston: Martinus Nijhoff Publishers.

McNamara, K. (2013). Seeking justice in Ugandan courts: Amnesty and the case of Thomas Kyowelo. *Washington University Global Studies Law Review, 12*, 653–671.

Moreno-Ocampo, L. (2011). The role of the international community in assisting the International Criminal Court to secure justice and accountability. In R. Provost & P. Akhavan (Eds.), *Confronting genocide* (pp. 279–290). New York: Springer.

Morrissey, P. (2012). Applied rights in international criminal law: Defence counsel and the right to disclosure. In G. Boas, W. A. Schabas & M. P. Scharf (Eds.), *International criminal justice: Legitimacy and coherence* (pp. 68–104). Northampton, MA: Edward Elgar.

Mueller, S. D. (2014). Kenya and the International Criminal Court (ICC): Politics, the election and the law. *Journal of East African Studies, 8*, 25–42.

Mundis, D. A. (2003). The Assembly of State Parties and the institutional framework of the International Criminal Court. *American Journal of International Law, 97*, 132–147.

Needham, J. (2011). Protection or prosecution for Omar Al-Bashir? The changing state of immunity in international criminal law. *Auckland University Law Review, 17*, 219–248.

Nerlich, V. (2012). The confirmation of charges procedure at the International Criminal Court. *Journal of International Criminal Justice, 10*, 1339–1356.

Office of the Prosecutor. (2014, December 2). *Report on preliminary examination activities. International Criminal Court.* Available at: http://www.icc-cpi.int/iccdocs/otp/OTP-Pre-Exam-2014.pdf.

Prunier, G. (2011). Darfur: Genocidal theory and practical atrocities. In R. Provost & P. Akhavan (Eds.), *Confronting genocide* (pp. 45–56). New York: Springer.

SáCouto, S. & Katherine C. (2014a). The adjudication process and reasoning at the International Criminal Court: The *Lubanga* Trial Chamber judgment, sentencing and reparations. In Y. Haeck & E. Brems (Eds.) *Human rights and civil liberties in the twenty-first century* (pp. 131–155). New York: Springer.

SáCouto, S. & Katherine C. T. (2014b). Regulation 55 and the rights of the accused at the International Criminal Court. *Human Rights Brief, 21*, 17–23.

Schabas, W. (2007). *An introduction to the International Criminal Court.* New York: Cambridge University Press, 3rd ed.

Scharf, M. P. (2012). Order in the courtroom: The unique challenge of maintaining control of a war crimes trial. In G. Boas, W. A. Schabas & M. P. Scharf (Eds.), *International criminal justice: Legitimacy and coherence* (pp. 25–43). Northampton, MA: Edward Elgar.

Shaw, G. J. (2012). Convicting inhumanity *in absentia*: Holding trials *in absentia* at the International Criminal Court. *George Washington International Law Review, 44*, 107–140.

Stegmiller, I. (2013). The International Criminal Court and Mali: Towards more transparency in international criminal law investigations? *Criminal Law Forum, 24*, 475–499.

Steinhauser, G. (2014, September 24). International Criminal Court opens second Central African Republic probe. *Wall Street Journal.* Available at: http://www.wsj.com/articles/international-criminal-court-opens-second-central-african-republic-probe-1411576898.

Stewart, D. (2014). *International criminal law in a nutshell.* St. Paul, MN: West Academic Publishing.

Tiemessen, A. 2014. The International Criminal Court and the politics of prosecutions. *International Journal of Human Rights, 18,* 444–461.

Trendafilova, E. (2009). Fairness and expeditiousness in the International Criminal Court's pre-trial proceedings. In C. Stahn & G. Sluiter (Eds.), *The emerging practice of the International Criminal Court* (pp. 441–458). Boston: Martinus Nijhoff Publishers.

van der Vyver, J. D. (2011). Prosecuting the President of Sudan: A dispute between the African Union and the International Criminal Court. *African Human Rights Law Journal, 11,* 683–698.

Vinck, P., & Pham, P. N. (2010). Outreach evaluation: The International Criminal Court in the Central African Republic. *International Journal of Transitional Justice, 4,* 421–442.

Wiersing, A. (2012). *Lubanga* and its implications for victims seeking reparations at the International Criminal Court. *Amsterdam Law Forum, 4,* 21–39.

Chapter 6
Sentencing, Punishment, and Appeals

Abstract This chapter will explore international criminal sentencing at the Trial Chamber and subsequent proceedings before the Appeals Chamber. The Rome Statute provides some boundaries for appropriate sentences, though it does not lay out guidelines. Consequently, this chapter discusses the risk of sentencing disparities among different panels of judges or with other international criminal tribunals. The chapter will also explore the range of punishment options that are available for international crimes, including transfer of a prisoner to a member country, issues related to early release or clemency, and the possibility of alternative sanctions for offenders.

Keywords Appeals · Death penalty · Fines · Imprisonment · Life imprisonment · Punishment · Reparations · Sentencing · Trust fund for victims

6.1 Sentencing

The International Criminal Court provides for a separate sentencing hearing at Article 76 of the Rome Statute, either on the Court's own motion or by request of the parties, to hear additional evidence or submissions relevant to the sentence. This is especially beneficial in a lengthy, complex, and highly emotional case. Although the ICTY and ICTR initially allowed separate sentencing hearings, as is typical in a common law proceeding, these were eventually abolished, perhaps for financial efficiency. This limits the tactical decisions that an accused can make at trial, because an accused who pleaded guilty may not wish to present evidence relevant to sentencing prior to a conviction so as not to prejudice the outcome. In addition, victim impact testimony, highly relevant to sentencing, may be poignant and disturbing and could prejudice the guilt inquiry (Keller 2001: 68–69, 73; Drumbl and Gallant 2002: 142). Unlike the trial itself, a sentencing hearing is more concerned with the victims' losses, and a separate sentencing hearing could be another means of involving victims in criminal proceedings before the Court in line with restorative justice principles.

Sentencing decisions of international criminal tribunals have articulated different sentencing philosophies or purposes, delineated different aggravating or mitigating factors, and taken the individual circumstances of the perpetrator into account in different ways. The foremost consideration in an international sentencing decision is typically the gravity or seriousness of an offense (Carcano 2002: 590). Problems of sentencing consistency are likely to worsen as the ICC case load increases (Henham 2003a: 93–94). Because international criminal tribunals are not specifically bound by prior precedent or decisions of *other* tribunals, the opportunity to develop a kind of "common law" of sentencing practice is limited (Pickard 1997: 129).

The Court's sentence in *Lubanga* of fourteen years for enlisting, conscripting, and using child soldiers in combat, minus six years for time served, was analyzed in a lengthy opinion. Although the Prosecutor sought the presumptive maximum sentence under the Rome Statute of thirty years' imprisonment, the Court considered the fact that most soldiers in the armed forces were adults and there was no evidence that a large number of soldiers were extremely young. In addition, as Kurth (2013: 449–450) explains, although the child soldiers were subject to punishment, such disciplinary actions were not found to be abusive or part of a systematic organizational policy directed by Lubanga himself. The Court also did not consider the sexual violence in the armed force as an aggravating factor, finding that the link between the defendant and sexual violence was not proven. Ultimately, they affixed the punishment of 12 years' imprisonment for enlistment of child soldiers, 13 years for conscription, and 15 years for active use in hostilities, emphasizing that actual *use* of child soldiers was the worst of the three crimes (ibid.: 451–452). Human rights observers and the Congolese government criticized the sentence as low in relation to the crimes, as, with six years of time served, he will be out of prison in less than eight years and eligible for early release even earlier (Dana 2014: 33–34).

6.1.1 Sentencing Consistency at Prior International Criminal Tribunals

At the Yugoslavia and Rwanda tribunals, the Court specified the gravity of the offense, the defendant's individual circumstances, aggravating and mitigating factors, and general sentencing practices of Rwanda and Yugoslavia as factors to be considered in crafting a sentence. However, the Yugoslavia tribunal only gave one life sentence out of 62 convictions, and dispensed sentences of 45 and 25 years, respectively, to Generals Tihomir Blaskić and Dario Kordić though both were convicted of crimes against humanity including persecution, murder, and inhumane acts (Stein 2014: 537–538). Inconsistent sentencing practices may decrease the overall legitimacy of the tribunals' work and reinforce the views of critics who believe that the enforcement of international criminal law is fatally arbitrary. Drumbl and Gallant (2002: 143) have identified sentences for crimes against humanity as particularly variable at the Yugoslavia tribunal, perhaps due to the tribunal's efforts to prosecute a broad range of individuals at different levels of the command structure. Some criminological studies, however, have found the Rwanda and Yugoslavia tribunals to impose roughly consistent sentences in the aggregate, determining that persons convicted of genocide are subject to more severe sentences than those convicted of crimes against humanity; high-ranking defendants are sentenced more harshly than low-ranking defendants; defendants convicted of multiple crimes receive more severe sentences; and mitigating and aggravating factors are correlated to sentence length (Holá et al. 2012: 548–549). However, Dana (2014: 103–106) describes how higher-ranking officials at the ICTY, who would ordinarily possess greater culpability, could benefit from disproportionately greater sentence reductions or early release when judges weighed mitigating factors such as whether the defendant pleaded guilty.

In addition to inconsistency at international criminal tribunals, scholars have debated the consistency among them. In particular, the sentences passed by the Yugoslavia tribunal were relatively lenient, while those passed by the Rwanda tribunal and the Special Court for Sierra Leone were comparatively harsher, with a much higher proportion of offenders sentenced to life imprisonment. According to an empirical analysis by Holá et al. (2011: 436–438), many more defendants at the Rwanda tribunal were senior-ranking government officials and organizers of violence who were charged with genocide, while a greater proportion of defendants at the Yugoslavia tribunal were lower-ranking, hands-on executioners of persecutory campaigns. This evidence may suggest an emerging hierarchy in international criminal law, with genocide ranking as the worst crime, followed by crimes against humanity and then war crimes. Carcano (2002: 607) adds that war crimes are typically perpetrated to achieve objectives of war, while crimes against humanity are exclusively conceived and perpetrated to harm civilians. Although all three tribunals were required to consider local sentencing practices in determining sentences, the differences in sentencing among domestic courts in Rwanda, Sierra Leone, and Yugoslavia are not enough to explain these disparities (Danner 2001: 441–443).

During sentencing, while the defense needs to prove mitigating factors beyond a preponderance of the evidence, the prosecution must prove aggravating factors beyond a reasonable doubt, a higher threshold (Beresford 2001: 55). Aggravating factors cited by the Yugoslavia and Rwanda tribunals have included the scope of the crime; number and suffering of the victims; form of participation in the crime, including direct involvement or premeditation; motive; and superior responsibility, among others. Mitigating factors have included a plea of guilty; personal circumstances, such as background, emotional state, or subsequent behavior; and superior orders (ibid: 54–82). The International Criminal Court may look to similar factors in its future sentencing jurisprudence.

6.1.2 Sentencing Consistency at the International Criminal Court

The International Criminal Court does not resolve the dilemma of inconsistent sentencing and may create several additional complications. Unlike the ICTY, the Rome Statute does not specifically refer to the sentencing practices of the territory where the crime was committed as a factor to be considered in determining sentence length (Glickman 2004: 255, 259). Because many jurisdictions have passed domestic legislation outlawing genocide, war crimes, or crimes against humanity, the Court could give deference to how the jurisdiction would have prosecuted the crime (Stein 2014: 558).

Part of the difficulty with crafting consistent sentences is that international criminal tribunals do not always articulate clear philosophies of punishment. International criminal punishment has different philosophical goals and justifications than domestic punishment. For instance, rehabilitation may be less important for perpetrators who have committed genocide or war crimes, while domestic sentencing is often less concerned about restorative justice principles or the considerations of victims (Henham 2003a: 89, 2003b: 80–81). Rehabilitation has never been highly significant in determining a sentence before an international criminal tribunal; rather, retribution and deterrence are the primary sentencing rationales cited in international criminal jurisprudence (Dana 2014: 48). However, Glickman (2004: 247–248, 254–255) called the sentences passed by ICTY "far too lenient" to actually reflect retributive justice. Despite lip service to retribution, Glickman explains, the judges relied heavily on individual mitigating factors, suggesting that they were influenced by other sentencing aims, perhaps deterrence or restorative justice. In addition, the sentences for genocide, war crimes, and crimes against humanity seem especially *low* when compared to most domestic jurisdictions' punishments for rape, homicide, and torture. As Heller (2012: 236–238) explains, many national jurisdictions punish offenders for rape and homicide with life imprisonment or possibly the death penalty, while a single instance of rape could be between 10 years imprisonment and life imprisonment in most jurisdictions. In looking at the different international tribunals he concludes that the additional gravity of international crimes makes almost no difference in sentencing practice compared to sentences for domestic crimes.

Without clear aims and justifications for punishment, some inconsistency may be expected as different judicial actors apply different sentencing philosophies. Should sentencing guidelines be proposed? One proposal would be to have ranges depending on the severity of the crime, such as one for genocide resulting in death, another for genocide not resulting in death, and a third for conspiracy to commit genocide (Pickard 1997: 141). It appears from sentence length alone that the ICTY and ICTR treated genocide most harshly, as the "crime of crimes" with a very high intent requirement, and considered crimes against humanity more serious than war crimes, perhaps because crimes against humanity must be widespread and systematic and are committed pursuant to an organized state or organizational policy, unlike war crimes (Glickman 2004: 260). Another proposal would be to adopt mandatory minimum sentences, which was considered at the Rome Conference, though this creates another dilemma of how to distinguish superior officials from lower-level perpetrators who were following orders from political and military leaders (ibid.: 263–264).

6.2 Punishment

The basic statutory punishment provision in the Rome Statute, Article 77, states that a sentence of imprisonment may not exceed 30 years. The provision contains an exception, meant to be rarely imposed, that a defendant could be sentenced to life imprisonment "when justified by the extreme gravity of the crime," a negotiated compromise that adds an undefined element into an otherwise consistent standard (Dana 2009: 914–915). The Rome Statute also enables the Court to impose a fine (but only in addition to imprisonment) and forfeiture of proceeds, property, or assets derived from the crime. The Court is required to deduct time served in detention, and, in the event that a defendant is convicted of more than one crime, the Court may not exceed 30 years or natural life for the total period of imprisonment (Schabas 2007: 318–20). The enforcement of sentences requires the cooperation of states parties. Although only the Court may alter a sentence, a state party is responsible for maintaining and inspecting prison conditions; paying for the costs of incarceration; recovering fines, property, or proceeds from sale; and transferring a prisoner at the conclusion of his or her sentence (Abtahi and Koh 2012: 11 *et seq.*).

6.2.1 Death Penalty

Although the Nuremberg and Tokyo trials could authorize the death penalty, the Yugoslavia and Rwanda tribunals were only entitled to impose life imprisonment as a maximum sentence. The International Criminal Court is also limited only to life imprisonment as a maximum sentence, and only if "justified by the extreme gravity of the crime," as noted in Article 77 of the Rome Statute. The debate over capital punishment threatened to unravel the Rome Conference, with Islamic and Caribbean states, along with Singapore and a handful of African countries, threatening the Conference's attempts at a consensus. In the end, the compromise was Article 80, which states that the Rome Statute's penalty provisions do not prejudice domestic criminal sanctions—in other words, if a state chooses to prosecute an international crime rather than submit the case to the Court, it is not bound by the penalty provisions of the Rome Statute. As Schabas writes, however, "the exclusion of the death penalty from the Rome Statute can be nothing but an important benchmark in an unquestionable trend towards universal abolition of capital punishment" (Schabas 2007: 313–16). International criminal tribunals have followed emerging international trends toward death penalty abolition and heightened skepticism toward sentences of life imprisonment.

Many domestic jurisdictions, however, have authorized capital punishment and life imprisonment for genocide, war crimes, and crimes against humanity. In countries such as the Democratic Republic of the Congo or Mali, both of which are the sites of ongoing ICC investigations, the death penalty for genocide and crimes against humanity has been proposed or enacted (Triponel and Pearson 2010: 96). This creates the odd situation, as after the Rwandan genocide, where middle-level perpetrators tried in national courts may be punished more harshly than senior-level perpetrators tried in international courts (Ohlin 2005: 748–749). Because international law still permits the death penalty, even if it is disfavored and subject to strict limitations, the International Criminal Court will likely respect the decision of states parties to retain the death penalty when it assesses whether an investigation or prosecution is genuine for purposes of complementarity (Abbas 2008: 44–45).

6.2.2 Life Imprisonment

The basic sentencing provision at Article 77 of the Rome Statute declares that the Court may impose imprisonment "for a specified number of years, which may not exceed a maximum of thirty years," but that it may impose life imprisonment when justified by the *extreme* gravity of the crime. The provision does not define "extreme gravity," but presumably the drafters of the Rome Statute envisioned something beyond the seriousness of the core crimes prosecuted by the Court. Article 77 allows the Court to sentence a defendant for up to 30 years *or* to natural life, not to a term of imprisonment beyond 30 years. This proposal elicited opposition from several European and Latin American countries, which were in principle opposed to life imprisonment or at least to life imprisonment without the possibility of parole or conditional release. For instance, objections came from Brazil and Portugal, where life imprisonment is unconstitutional; both countries had to overcome domestic opposition on this point in order to ratify the Rome Statute (Schabas 2007: 316–17; Dana 2009: 914–915). The idea to include a maximum term for a sentence of determinate years originated with France and other civil law countries to increase legal certainty with regard to the range of imprisonment (Dana 2009: 913).

6.2.3 Enforcement of a Sentence

The basic enforcement structure of a criminal sentence at Article 103 is that a state must first be placed on a list of states willing to enforce sentences and then must accept the President of the Court's designation in an individual case. This state then becomes the "state of enforcement." When exercising discretion to designate a state of enforcement, the Presidency must consider, among other factors, equitable distribution of prisoners, international treaty standards governing prison conditions, and the views and nationality of the prisoner. If the Court cannot designate a particular state of enforcement, the host state (the Netherlands) will accept the prisoner, as governed by the Headquarters Agreement (Abtahi and

Koh 2012: 4, 6–10). This is similar to the Rwanda and Yugoslavia tribunals. The Rwanda tribunal's statute stated that imprisonment was to be served in Rwanda or any state that indicated a willingness to accept defendants, such as Mali; imprisonment was to be in accordance with the laws of that state subject to the supervision of the tribunal. Prisoners from the tribunal for Yugoslavia were transferred to third countries, including Austria, Finland, Germany, Norway, and Spain (Drumbl and Gallant 2002: 141).

The sentence is binding on the state of enforcement and the state cannot alter it or release a defendant before the sentence expires. The Court, however, is empowered to release a defendant after a portion of the sentence has been served. This is not parole or conditional release; the decision to free the prisoner is final and irreversible. This is to reward defendants who assist the Court in later prosecutions or in victim reparations (Schabas 2007: 318–20). The Appeals Chamber will consider a reduction either when the person has served two-thirds of his or her sentence or, in the case of life imprisonment, after the person has served 25 years, in accordance with Article 110 (Abtahi and Koh 2012: 11). After completion of a sentence, a prisoner may be transferred to his or her home country or any other country that agrees to accept him or her. This includes extradition for prosecution for other crimes, including those committed during incarceration (Schabas 2007: 320–22). Enforcement of fines, forfeiture measures, and reparation orders work in a similar manner; states parties must cooperate with orders issued by the President of the Court, including transferring property or proceeds of sale to the Court. The Court will ensure that fines, property, and proceeds are transferred to or deposited in the Trust Fund or provided to relevant victims. A convicted person who fails to pay an imposed fine may be subject to an extension of his or her term of imprisonment (Abtahi and Koh 2012: 20–22).

The Rome Statute states that the state of enforcement shall not release a convicted criminal before the sentence expires, and that the Court alone should have the right to decide a reduction of sentence. The Court thus has direct authority to set minimum penalties and early release rather than leaving these decisions in the hands of the state enforcing the sentence. Sentence variation at the ICTY and other international criminal tribunals was exacerbated by the fact that convicted war criminals benefited from early release provisions in their respective countries of incarceration. Final decisions for early release rested with the states of enforcement. The ICTY Appeals Chamber stated that a convicted prisoner should serve a minimum of two thirds of the sentence, but it proved difficult to enforce (Glickman 2004: 257–258). The Rome Statute corrected many of these shortcomings that placed final authority over parole and commutation in the hands of the states of enforcement (ibid.: 265–267). Nonetheless, corrections systems have other variations of course; prison conditions, for instance, are more tolerable in some countries than in others. The Rome Statute specifies that conditions for imprisonment must be equivalent to those of others in the state who have been convicted of similar offenses; the Court has also required states of enforcement to allow inspections of prison conditions (Abtahi and Koh 2012: 12–13).

6.3 Reparations to Victims

As part of the Court's restorative justice mission, the International Criminal Court allows victims of crimes that fall within its jurisdiction the right to file applications for reparations. No such right existed at other international tribunals, and there is no precedent for reparations awarded to individual victims from individual offenders in the course of international criminal proceedings. However, victims of atrocity have in the past received reparations from *governments*. In addition, corporations complicit in human rights abuses have provided legal settlements to victims. The Conference on Jewish Material Claims against Germany, for instance, represents the Jewish world in negotiating compensation, providing support services, and recovering stolen property for victims of the Holocaust (Dwertmann 2010: 1, 9, 22). The Rome Statute gives unlimited discretion to the Court to determine whether reparations should be paid, and the size and form of the reparation orders. Reparation comes in three types: restitution for actual losses, compensation for economic losses, and rehabilitation for helping a victim reintegrate into society. The Statute and Rules allow for the inclusion not only of direct victims, but also of persons indirectly harmed, such as family members and victim's organizations. The Statute also gives priority to awards for the benefit of children, elderly persons, persons with disabilities, and victims of sexual and gender-based violence (ibid.: 295–298; Garkawe 2012: 291–292; Henzelin 2006: 330–332).

The International Criminal Court's emphasis on restorative justice principles encompassing restitution, compensation, and rehabilitation for victims was the culmination of a long-term international trend. The ICTY and ICTR had rudimentary regimes that in theory allowed the tribunals to order restitution of property or proceeds, but victims had no standing themselves to bring claims. Though the governing statute authorized restitution and compensation, no claims were ever awarded; most were transferred to national authorities. The ICTR did provide victims of sexual assault with counseling, anti-retroviral treatment for HIV/AIDS, and general medical services for the period in which the victims were participating in proceedings, and both the ICTR and ICTY had voluntary trust funds that were used in part for victim support (De Brouwer 2007: 214–218).

In addition to claims dating to the Holocaust era, other important experiments in international mass claims processes for victims have included the Iran-United States Claims Tribunal established in The Hague to compensate Americans for monetary losses as a result of the Iranian Revolution and hostage crisis; the United Nations Compensation Commission, which processes individual claims for reparations as a result of Iraq's unlawful invasion of Kuwait in 1991; and compensation from Libya for state sponsorship of terror, including to the families of victims of the bombing of Pan Am Flight 103 over Lockerbie, Scotland, in 1988. In each of these cases, victims were allowed to make individual claims for losses, and a variety of methods were employed to calculate the amount of restitution. For instance, the UN Compensation Commission divided losses into three categories: "A" (for individuals forced to leave Iraq or Kuwait); "B" (for those who suffered serious personal injury or death); and "C" (for those who suffered personal losses of up to $100,000). Claims in Category "B" were relatively few in number and reviewed on a case by case basis, while claims in Categories "A" and "C" involved computerized verification, sampling, individual review, and, for category "C," statistical modeling. This provides a template for how large numbers of claims may be handled expeditiously by an international tribunal in the future (Henzelin et al. 2006: 342).

The existence of a victim reparations mechanism at the Court is an attempt to make the victim the central focus of the criminal proceeding. Whether the prospect of paying individual reparations to victims will serve as a deterrent to future crimes is difficult to say, but the compensatory mechanism at the Court is a revolutionary development in international law. Potentially, individual reparations could reduce harm to victims, restore individual dignity of assist with reintegration into society, and trigger or support a broader process of societal reconciliation (Dwertmann 2010: 41–42). Given the possibility for large numbers of claimants for compensation at the ICC, the Court is likely to adopt strict criteria for claims. Determining eligibility and informing potential victims of the right to seek compensation will be a challenging task; the burden will be on the claimant to establish that the damage suffered was the result of the criminal conduct of the convicted person (Henzelin et al. 2006: 328–329).

The Rome Statute only permits individual perpetrators to pay compensation to victims. The Statute does not authorize governments or corporations to provide compensation to victims, even where these entities bear some responsibility for the crimes (though the Security Council may seize state assets for the purpose of satisfying reparation claims). However, Article 79 of the Rome Statute creates an independent organ known as the Trust Fund for Victims, which receives voluntary contributions from governments, international organizations, corporations, and individuals for the benefit of victims of mass crimes. Because this fund is independent of the prosecution, it is not tied to the specific culpability of a perpetrator or a perpetrator's financial ability to provide reparations. Although the Trust Fund is distinct from the Rome Statute's reparations provisions, Trust Fund assistance nonetheless has reparatory effects for victims. Contributors to the Fund can earmark portions of their contributions. In 2008, the total amount of available Trust Fund resources was over $3,000,000. Although a considerable sum has been raised from voluntary contributions by states, presumably little or nothing has been collected from defendants as individual reparations (Dwertmann 2010: 285–287; Garkawe 2012: 291).

This system of reparations has some obvious limitations. Perpetrators of serious crimes probably do not accumulate substantial property or wealth, and even if they did, it is not clear that the Court will have the ability to secure the property or wealth for redistribution. Furthermore, in an era of increasing donor fatigue, one might wonder whether it is realistic to raise voluntary contributions sufficient to satisfy tens of thousands of potential victims of mass violence. Article 79 has already created expectations among victims and their advocates, however, and disappointing these expectations may affect the Court's legitimacy (Arsanjani and Reisman 2005: 401–402). In addition to the forms of reparations mentioned above, the Rome Statute specifies additional assistance to victims of sexual violence in particular. Building on the previous experience of the ICTR, the Trust Fund makes possible interim relief for victims as early as the investigation phase, providing physical and psychological rehabilitation and material support to victims of sexual trauma. This support may include anti-retroviral drugs for HIV/AIDS and other reproductive health services. This is the only instance in which relief to victims can be made during the criminal proceeding and before conviction (De Brower 2007: 230–231).

In the *Lubanga* case, which involved recruitment for child soldiers, the Court was required to frame who the victims actually were, which affected who was eligible for compensation. This produced a danger that the Court would limit reparations to "direct victims," that is, child soldiers themselves and their families, and not to "indirect victims" such as those harmed by the use of child soldiers in conflict. The Court declined to limit reparations only to "direct victims." The Court emphasized, however, that the claimants for reparations must establish a nexus, or relationship, between the harm and the defendant himself; that is, the claimants must show that the defendant himself was responsible in some way for the harm. Those victimized by child soldiers in the conflict may not be eligible for compensation if the incidents were not planned, directed, or orchestrated by the defendant (Amman 2012: 814–815; Wiersing 2012: 29–30). Though not eligible for reparations, the communities of those victimized by Lubanga's crimes, however, may still benefit from contributions from the Trust Fund, even without establishing a nexus to Lubanga himself.

6.4 The Appeals Chamber

Like the ICTY and ICTR (but unlike the Nuremberg and Tokyo tribunals), the International Criminal Court provides a system of appeal to a separate chamber. Since the 1960s, international human rights instruments increasingly recognize the right to appeal as a fundamental due process right for criminal defendants. The Rome Statute goes beyond these minimum guarantees. The Appeals Chamber sits as the third division of judicial decision-making, along with the Pre-Trial and Trial Chambers. An appeal against a decision of acquittal or conviction or against a sentence can be brought by the Prosecutor or by a convicted person. However, the Prosecutor may only appeal against an error of fact or law, procedural error, or an excessive sentence; a convicted person may appeal against any of these or any other ground that affects the fairness or reliability of the proceedings. The Appeals Chamber has the ability to reverse or amend the decision or the sentence, or order a new trial before a different Trial Chamber. If necessary, the Appeals Chamber may permit the introduction of new evidence. The Appeals Chamber is also able to hear interlocutory appeals, that is, appeals raised during the course of proceedings that could affect the outcome of the case or the rights of the parties, such as evidentiary or jurisdictional disputes. These types of appeals may come from either the Pre-Trial Chamber or the Trial Chamber, and are settled by a majority of judges. Appeals judges may also revise a sentence based on new evidence or discovery that trial evidence was false or forged. The Rome Statute does not specifically provide for reconsideration of a decision of the Appeals Chamber in the event of an error of fact or law, but a process may be established in the future. A defendant who was wrongly convicted and punished is also entitled to compensation (De Cesari 2001: 225–230; Schabas 2007: 306–311).

6.5 Discussion Questions

1. What theoretical and practical difficulties do you see with the reparations regime established by the Rome Statute? Do you believe it will be successful?
2. What are the problems of and possible solutions for sentencing inconsistencies at international criminal tribunals? Are there any alternative sentences to incarceration that should be considered?

6.6 Further Reading

For an in-depth analysis of sentencing at international criminal tribunals, see Silvia D'Ascoli, *Sentencing in International Criminal Law: The UN Ad Hoc Tribunals and Future Perspectives for the ICC* (Hart Publishing 2011). The book compares sentencing regimes at the ICTY, ICTR, and International Criminal Court, and draws out guiding principles for sentencing decisions. For more on victim participation and reparations, Luke Moffett's book *Justice for Victims Before the International Criminal Court* (Routledge 2014) is instructive, and includes a detailed case study on Northern Uganda.

References

Abbas, G. (2008, Nov 23). The adequacy of Uganda's war crimes court (Public International Law and Policy Group). Available at: http://law.case.edu/Academics/AcademicCenters/Cox/WarCrimesResearchPortal/show_document.asp?id=172.

Abtahi, H., & Koh, S. A. (2012). The emerging enforcement practice of the International Criminal Court. *Cornell International Law Journal, 45*, 1–23.

Amman, D. M. (2012). *Prosecutor v. Lubanga. American Journal of International Law, 106*(4), 809–817.

Arsanjani, M., & Reisman, W. M. (2005). The law-in-action of the International Criminal Court. *American Journal of International Law, 99*, 385–403.

Beresford, S. (2001). Unshackling the paper tiger: The sentencing practices of the ad hoc International Criminal Tribunals for the Former Yugoslavia and Rwanda. *International Criminal Law Review, 1*, 33–90.

Carcano, A. (2002). Sentencing and the gravity of the offence in international criminal law. *International and Comparative Law Quarterly, 51*, 583–609.

Dana, S. (2009). Beyond retroactivity to realizing justice: A theory on the principle of legality in international criminal law sentencing. *Journal of Criminal Law and Criminology, 99*, 857–927.

Dana, S. (2014). The limits of judicial idealism: Should the International Criminal Court engage with consequentialist aspirations? *Penn State Journal of Law and International Affairs, 3*, 30–112.

Danner A. M. (2001) Constructing a Hierarchy of Crimes in International Criminal Law Sentencing, *Virginia Law Review, 87*, 415–501 (2001).

De Brouwer, A. M. (2007). Reparation to victims of sexual violence: Possibilities at the International Criminal Court and at the trust fund for victims and their families. *Leiden Journal of International Law, 20*, 207–237.

De Cesari, P. (2001). Observations on appeal before the International Criminal Court. In M. Politi & G. Nesi (Eds.), *The rome statute of the International Criminal Court: A challenge to impunity* (pp. 225–234). Burlington, VT: Ashgate Dartmouth.

Drumbl, M. A., & Gallant, S. K. (2002). Sentencing policies and practices in the international criminal tribunals. *Federal Sentencing Reporter, 15*, 140–144.

Dwertmann, E. (2010). *The reparation system of the International Criminal Court: Its implementation, possibilities, and limitations.* Boston: Martinus Nijhoff Publishers.

Garkawe, S. (2012). Have recent changes designed to benefit victims of international crimes added to the legitimacy of international criminal justice? In G. Boas, W. Schabas, & M. P. Scharf (Eds.), *International criminal justice: Legitimacy and coherence* (pp. 269–303). Northamton, MA: Edward Elgar.

Glickman, S. (2004). Victims' justice: Legitimizing the sentencing regime of the International Criminal Court. *Columbia Journal of Transnational Law, 43*, 229–268.

Heller, K. J. (2012). A sentencing-based theory of complementarity. *Harvard International Law Journal, 53*, 202–249.

Henham, R. (2003a). Some issues for sentencing in the International Criminal Court. *International and Comparative Law Quarterly, 52*(1), 81–114.

Henham, R. (2003b). The philosophical foundations of international sentencing. *Journal of International Criminal Justice, 1*, 64–85.

Henzelin, M., Heiskanen, V., & Mettraux, G. (2006). Reparations to victims before the International Criminal Court: Lessons from international mass claims processes. *Criminal Law Forum, 17*, 317–344.

Holá, B., Smeulers, A., & Bijleveld, C. (2011). International sentencing facts and figures. *Journal of International Criminal Justice, 9*, 411–439.

Holá, B., Bijleveld, C., & Smeulers, A. (2012). Consistency of international sentencing: ICTY and ICTR case study. *European Journal of Criminology, 9*, 539–552.

Keller, A. N. (2001). Punishment for violations of international criminal law: An analysis of sentencing at the ICTY and ICTR. *Indiana International and Comparative Law Review, 12*, 53–74.

Kurth, M. E. (2013). The *Lubanga* case of the International Criminal Court: A critical analysis of the Trial Chamber's findings on issues of active use, age, and gravity. *Goettingen Journal of International Law, 5*, 431–453.

Ohlin, J. D. (2005). Applying the death penalty to crimes of genocide. *American Journal of International Law, 99*, 747–777.

Pickard, D. B. (1997). Proposed sentencing guidelines for the International Criminal Court. *Loyola Los Angeles International and Comparative Law Review, 20*, 123–164.

Schabas, W. (2007). *An introduction to the International Criminal Court* (3rd ed.). New York: Cambridge University Press.

Stein, A. J. (2014). Reforming the sentencing regime for the most serious crimes of concern: The International Criminal Court through the lens of the Lubanga trial. *Brooklyn Journal of International Law, 39*, 521–562.

Triponel, A., & Pearson, S. (2010). African states and the International Criminal Court: A silent revolution in international criminal law. *Journal of Law and Social Challenges, 12*, 65–106.

Wiersing, A. (2012). *Lubanga* and its implications for victims seeking reparations at the International Criminal Court. *Amsterdam Law Forum, 4*, 21–39.

Chapter 7
Current Controversies

Abstract This chapter will explore pressing issues facing the International Criminal Court, such as the perceived targeting of the continent of Africa and the poor relations between the Court and the African Union. In addition, the special case of Palestine will be discussed, as the Israeli-Palestinian conflict will be a source of controversy in coming years. Finally, this chapter will look at the role of local criminal justice processes in the Court's operations, especially as to the principle of complementarity.

Keywords Africa · African Union · Customary criminal justice · *Gacaca* · Israel · *Mato oput* · *Nahe biti* · Palestine

7.1 The Court's "Africa" Problem

The Rome Statute came into force during the wave of democratization and improved transparency that swept across the African continent in the 1990s; this was also the era, however, of brutal internal conflicts and state collapse as crumbing regimes succumbed to economic austerity and civil strife. In April 1999, the Organization of African Unity (later the African Union) called on all African states to ratify the Rome Statute. However, ten years later, the African Union encouraged member states not to cooperate with the International Criminal Court because of a perceived targeting of the continent in case selection and prosecution (Mills 2012: 405). The Court was unprepared for the backlash from the African Union criticizing its involvement in Darfur, Sudan, and the imbroglio over the Kenyan election violence case. To be sure, the African Union is not a monolithic body. While some political leaders have sought to preserve their sovereignty, others have been more accepting of human rights principles. In addition, Fatou Bensouda, herself an African, may have a better relationship with the African continent than her predecessor as Prosecutor, Luis Moreno Ocampo. African delegations lobbied heavily for Bensouda's selection in the Assembly of States Parties. The continent of Africa felt sidelined by the power politics of the Security Council's Sudan referral and by the Kenyan investigation, though this was less true for Libya, where Gaddafi was isolated and even the African members of the Council voted for the resolution (ibid.: 440–447). In addition, despite early indications that African countries would readily embrace the Court, they were slow to enact implementing legislation that made it possible for the government to cooperate with the tribunal and domestically prosecute the four core crimes (Bekou and Shah 2006: 501–504).

The most obvious defense of the Court's conduct is that the continent of Africa includes several intractable conflicts, including a large, self-reinforcing conflict system that spans the Congo basin and reaches into the Central African Republic, Chad, northern Uganda, and Sudan. Besides being the site of serious atrocity crimes, the violence has also tended to weaken these states' capacities to investigate and prosecute international crimes (Nkhata 2011: 281–282). Mendes (2010: 35–36, 168) is critical of the position of African countries that the Court is biased against the Global South and reckless as to the potential for peaceful settlement of violent conflicts in Africa. He notes that African countries were among the first to ratify the Rome Statute and in sheer numbers constitute the largest regional bloc of states parties. Five of the pending situations were referred to the Court by African governments themselves, and the situation in Kenya, the first *proprio motu* investigation, initially had the full blessing of the government. As for Sudan, Mendes argues that the Court showed impartiality in investigating not only President Omar al-Bashir, but also one of the rebel leaders in Darfur, Bahr Idriss Abu Garda, although the Court's judges ultimately did not confirm the charges against him (ibid.: 44). At least 47 African countries participated at the Rome Conference, including many as members of the Like-Minded Group. Prominent among these was South Africa, a supporter of the Court, which even refused to sign a bilateral immunity agreement with the United States. Domestically, South Africa was the first African country to pass full implementing legislation, the International Criminal Court Act, to create a domestic framework for cooperation with the Court, which has served as a model law for other African countries. Nonetheless, South Africa had an ambiguous position on the arrest warrant for President al-Bashir in Sudan, joining the African Union in calling for the withdrawal of the warrant (Stone 2011: 307–308, 323–326; Clarke 2009: 72). Another prominent critic of the International Criminal Court's African prosecutions is President Paul Kagame of Rwanda, which perhaps surprisingly is not a state party to the Rome Statute given the role the Rwandan genocide played in formulating the current international justice regime. However, Kagame had a similarly ambiguous relationship with the Rwanda tribunal. He has called the ICC a fraudulent institution created for poor African states as a form of imperialism aimed at control (Cole 2013: 15).

African criticism of the Court is not based solely on the cases on the Court's docket, but also on the cases that the Court has not taken. The Prosecutor has had a tendency to shy away from more politically difficult cases in favor of ones that are more palatable to the major powers, and in practice this means African cases. In the world of major power politics, this may have been a prudent course for a new institution as fragile as the Court. But it may come at a political cost. Many

African governments view the ICC as a hegemonic tool used by Western powers to bully states from the Global South and the indictments of Sudanese officials in particular as insufficiently sensitive to the peace process in Darfur (Reinold 2012: 1089). The African Union's proposal to the UN Security Council to defer the prosecution of Sudanese officials pending resolution of the peace process did not even receive serious consideration, even though the Security Council willingly passed a deferral for American troops serving as UN peacekeepers (ibid: 1098). After the Security Council failed to act, the African Union's objections centered on Article 16, the provision authorizing the Security Council to defer an investigation for a one-year renewable period. African states proposed an amendment to the Rome Statute allowing the UN General Assembly to consider a deferral request when the Security Council fails to do so. The unavoidable problem with Article 16, of course, is that it incorporates into the Rome Statute the inequitable distribution of power on the Security Council, especially through the veto held by the five permanent powers (Jalloh et al. 2011: 8–9).

In an effort to find "African solutions to African problems," the African Union Assembly sought to empower a regional court to try serious crimes of international concern, including genocide, crimes against humanity, and war crimes, which would be complementary to national jurisdiction. The result was the Protocol on Amendments to the Protocol on the Statute of the African Court of Justice and Human Rights, which would reorganize the African Court and add criminal jurisdiction to its mandate. Organized into pre-trial, trial, and appeals chambers, the African Court would be competent to try the same four core crimes as under the Rome Statute, as well as unconstitutional changes of government, piracy, terrorism, mercenarism, corruption, money laundering, human and drug trafficking, trafficking in hazardous waste, and illicit exploitation of natural resources (Martin and Bröhmer 2012: 254–257). In July 2014, the African Union Assembly adopted an amendment to the Protocol that would immunize African leaders from criminal prosecution before the proposed African Court. Article 46A-*bis* of the Protocol now states that "[n]o charges shall be commenced or continued before the Court against any serving African Union Head of State or Government, or anybody acting or entitled to act in such capacity, or other senior state officials based on their functions, during their tenure of office." Over 40 civil society groups expressed disapproval at the inclusion of immunity for heads of state and senior officials in the mandate of the new African Court (International Justice Resource Center 2014).

If implemented, the African Court of Justice and Human Rights would be the first international court to combine cases involving state responsibility for human rights violations with cases involving individual responsibility for criminal violations, distinct functions that require different evidentiary standards and enforcement mechanisms. The prosecutor would be independent and the African Court would respect the principle of complementarity. Whether the International Criminal Court would cooperate with the new institution, however, remains unanswered. Although the Rome Statute pledges to respect *national* prosecutions, it says nothing of *regional* prosecutions for purposes of complementarity.

Overlapping jurisdiction could result in dual prosecutions for the same conduct and could cause states to violate their obligations under the Rome Statute, by, for instance, transferring defendants to the African Court when they are obliged to transfer them to The Hague. In addition, although the Rome Statute can reach non-member states by Security Council referral, the African Court would only bind member states (Martin and Bröhmer 2012: 259–264).

The "Africa problem" unexpectedly affected the Court's legitimacy in the Global South among perhaps the Court's largest and most committed bloc of states parties. Yet, the Sudan referral in particular was precisely the type of case for which the Rome Statute contemplated Security Council referral: Sudan simply had not shown good faith in negotiating over the Darfur conflict and took no meaningful steps to combat the impunity of the perpetrators despite overwhelming support in the international community (Jalloh et al. 2011: 42–43). In other words, the system worked precisely as intended. Clarke (2009) presents a more fundamental critique of the International Criminal Court beyond objections against the Rome Statute itself and the cases that the Court has selected to pursue. In essence, the international justice project as a whole casts "black" bodies as helpless victims and "white" lawyers as saviors to protect Africans from themselves, supported by large amounts of financial capital from the Global North through development aid and lending while simultaneously ignoring the abuses committed in Africa by multinational corporations, arms manufacturers, and mercenaries from the Global North. Despite considerable African support for the international justice project given the weakness of domestic legal institutions and the problem of impunity, the North-South nature of the ICC and international justice generally may tend to reinforce Africa's subordinate position in international relations.

7.2 Palestine

Though it ultimately voted against the Rome Statute, Israel was an early supporter of the International Criminal Court and actively participated at the Rome Conference. On December 31, 2000, Israel joined the United States in signing the Rome Statute (Blumenthal 2002: 593). Like the United States, however, Israel subsequently "unsigned." Israel's main objection is that its settlement activity in the occupied territories has been targeted as a prosecutable war crime. The Rome Statute defines "war crimes" to include the indirect transfer of a state's own civilian population into the territories it occupies, which could leave vulnerable individuals living in Israeli settlements in Palestine. International law has never definitively settled the question of whether the Israeli occupation of Palestine is legal, and Israel argues that it captured the occupied territories of West Bank and the Gaza Strip from other occupying powers in the 1967 defensive war, as these territories were unallocated portions of the British Mandate and therefore not legally part of any country (Levy 1999: 208–209, 239–247). The Golan Heights region along the Syrian border may also be considered "occupied" for the same reason, though Syria is not a Court member.

Like the United States, Israel expressed concern over the Court's ability to prosecute non-members and for the broad definition of the crime of aggression. Israel and its allies perceive the country to be a potential target of a political Court prosecution (Blumenthal 2002: 605–607).

Once Israel withdrew from the Rome Statute, the Court did not possess jurisdiction over Israeli settlement activity. Although there were dual nationals and nationals of states that ratified the Rome Statute who were in the Israeli government and could therefore fall within the Court's jurisdiction, this source of personal jurisdiction was marginal. However, if the Court recognized Palestine as an independent state distinct from Israel and capable of ratifying the Rome Statute, Israel would be deeply vulnerable, especially considering the enormous level of potential liability on both sides of the Israeli-Palestinian conflict since July 1, 2002. Although the Rome Statute uses the word "state" several times, it does not define the term. An extensive academic and legal debate centered on whether Palestine qualified generally as a state under customary international law principles. At the Rome Conference, Palestine was not treated as a state, but as an observer (Mendes 2010: 180–181). Palestine possesses some but not all attributes of statehood, including varying degrees of membership in international organizations, but Shaw (2011: 319) notes that Israel retains several important powers, including the conduct of foreign relations for the West Bank and Gaza Strip. He argues that Palestine does not have the legal capacity to enter into international agreements such as the Rome Statute.

On January 22, 2009, the Palestinian Minister of Justice lodged an Article 12(3) declaration giving the Court ad hoc jurisdiction for "acts committed on the territory of Palestine since July 1, 2002." As noted earlier, Article 12(3) of the Rome Statute allows a type of self-referral by *non*-members in which they can consent to the Court's jurisdiction without ratifying the Statute, though it does not trigger an automatic investigation. Three years later, on April 3, 2012, the Office of the Prosecutor concluded that Palestine was still an "observer" in the UN General Assembly rather than a "Non-member State," and since the UN did not recognize Palestinian statehood, Palestine could not make an Article 12(3) declaration. In addition, it was not clear that Article 12(3) could apply retroactively, especially for an alleged "continuing" crime that predated the Rome Statute (Zimmermann 2013: 304–305, 311–312). On the other hand, Pellet (2010: 993–995) writes that Israel does not generally claim territorial sovereignty over the occupied territories. Failing to recognize the territory of Palestine for purposes of Article 12(3) would mean that no state could grant jurisdiction to the Court within these territories, which is contrary to the intention of the Rome Statute. On November 29, 2012, the UN General Assembly resolved the ambiguity when it voted to accord Palestine "non-member observer State" status in the United Nations by a vote of 138 to 9, with 41 abstentions. As a result, according to the International Criminal Court, Palestine became eligible to accept the Court's jurisdiction (Zimmerman 2013: 304).

Palestine's attempts to join the Rome Statute have threatened to undermine the Court's legitimacy among key constituencies, though the Arab world (except for Jordan) has largely remained outside of the Rome Statute, unlike the African continent. In November 2014, the Prosecutor announced that she would not pursue charges against Israeli officials for the attack on the Turkish flotilla the *M/V Mavi Mamara* when it attempted to break an Israeli blockade on the Gaza Strip coast, leading to an assault in which nine Turkish activists were killed. Although Turkey is not a member of the Court, the Court had personal jurisdiction based on the national flag flown on the vessel at the time of the attack, that of the Comoros Islands. In considering the request of the Comoros Islands to investigate, the Prosecutor announced that the alleged crime was not of "sufficient gravity" and therefore not admissible (BBC News 2014). A month later, on December 8, 2014, Palestine became an observer at the Assembly of States Parties based on its "upgraded" status at the United Nations (Sengupta 2014). Human rights observers such as Amnesty International have stated that both sides were potentially guilty of war crimes during the Gaza War in the summer of 2014: Israel for engaging in insufficiently discriminating attacks on dense residential complexes, and the Palestinian group Hamas for launching uncontrollable rocket attacks at civilian areas and using human shields during the fighting (Guardian 2014a).

On December 31, 2014, Palestine acceded to the Rome Statute, sparking international controversy including the suspension of some foreign aid to Palestine (Guardian 2014b). The President of the Palestinian Authority, Mahmoud Abbas, was under heavy diplomatic pressure after the Gaza War, the collapse of peace talks, Israeli restriction on Palestinian access to Jerusalem, and the failure of the UN Security Council to approve a resolution calling for an end to the occupation of Palestine. Under the Rome Statute's window period, Palestinian membership in the Rome Statute will be effective April 1, 2015 (Tait 2015). Palestine's declaration accepting the Court's jurisdiction was retroactive to June 13, 2014, which avoided the difficult question of whether Palestine could retroactively grant the Court jurisdiction before November 29, 2012 when its status was "upgraded" at the United Nations (ICC 2014). After April 1, 2015, the Office of the Prosecutor will face pressure to investigate Israeli (and Palestinian) conduct during the Gaza War in July and August 2014.

7.3 Consideration of Local Justice Mechanisms

One unresolved question posed by the Rome Statute is the extent to which the complementarity principle will embrace or resist non-Western or traditional forms of criminal justice. On the one hand, local criminal justice mechanisms have legitimacy among their populations, perhaps more than a distant and foreign tribunal. On the other hand, these justice methods may not accord with Western notions of due process for defendants and may not provide the same rights to women and children that they do to men. The International Criminal Court has faced criticism for being insufficiently sensitive to local justice mechanisms short of actual prosecutions. At the Rome Conference, for instance, the delegation of South Africa sought explicit recognition of truth and reconciliation commissions in lieu of national prosecutions under the complementarity principle (Robinson 2006: 226). The compromise that resulted in Article 17, the complementarity provision, allows the Court to consider whether a procedure is a "genuine" effort to do justice short of actual prosecution.

Given the Court's emphasis on restorative justice principles, however, local or traditional criminal justice methods may "complement" the Court's prosecutions. In lieu of criminal prosecutions, restorative or transitional justice mechanisms may provide non-adversarial ways of conducting investigations, establishing facts, determining accountability, and promoting social healing and forgiveness. They can furnish an opportunity for victims and even perpetrators to help establish the factual record of atrocities, recommend compensation, and formulate reforms to break a cycle of violence. Granting amnesties may encourage former perpetrators to come forward (Stewart 2014: 177). The Rome Statute would seem to allow South African-style truth commissions, because such commissions are not undertaken to shield perpetrators from accountability, but in order to promote a restorative conception of justice by emphasizing the importance of truth, reconciliation, and healing. Even if the Prosecutor were to go ahead with a prosecution where a perpetrator has participated in a truth commission process, the defense could still argue that such a prosecution would not be in the interests of justice. Certainly, trials have some advantages over truth commissions; their dramatic and compelling proceedings may aid the process of truth-telling and collective memory. However, research continually shows that many victims would prefer to participate in informal processes over a formal trial. The Prosecutor would likely consider support for a truth commission, the inclusiveness of proceedings, and the link to broader legal or social justice reform in determining whether the complementarity principle is satisfied (Roche 2005: 568–572).

One of the most famous types of local or traditional justice mechanisms is the *gacaca* process used after the Rwandan genocide. Named after a type of grass in Rwanda, *gacaca* refers to a system of customary dispute resolution dispensed on patches of grass, a type of informal small claims court in which village elders mediated disputes over water, livestock, or land. *Gacaca* proceedings were not established rituals before 1994, and they were not originally established to deal with such complex cases as criminal liability for genocide; the process was based on unwritten law and intended to reestablish social cohesion rather than to dispense punishment. The Government of Rwanda officially inaugurated the *gacaca* process in 2002, which accompanied the provisional release of low-level offenders to undergo the process. Judges were required to be Rwandan nationals over 21 years old without previous criminal convictions or suspicion of having participated in the genocide; they must also be honest and trustworthy. In addition, they could not be elected officials, lawyers, government or NGO employees, or members of the police, armed forces, or clergy. This was to ensure that the process is truly citizen-run without political or legal interference. The *gacaca* sentencing scheme allowed sentence reduction with confessions or where offenders were under 18 years old at the time of the crimes. Unlike under pre-colonial conceptions of *gacaca*, the judges focused specifically on eliciting testimony from those who are reluctant to testify, such as women and the young (Clarke 2009: 775–778, 789–794).

Like South Africa's Truth and Reconciliation Commission, the success of *gacaca* depended on the quality of the confessions elicited. From a practical perspective, *gacaca* offered an opportunity to winnow the nation's enormous prison population, though the *gacaca* system was resource-constrained and dependent on volunteers. Those who admitted to killing and who were thought to have recounted the details of their role in the genocide with sufficient remorse could see sentences reduced; by contrast, the later a confession came in the process, the smaller the reduction of sentence. If nobody came forward to offer evidence, a suspect was released (Temple-Raston 2005: 133–138). The *gacaca* process emphasized the community's ownership of and direct involvement in the post-conflict reconciliation process.

Another example of a local or customary criminal justice mechanism is the *mato oput* process among the Acholi people of northern Uganda, where social cohesion and trust are fractured after decades of conflict. The *mato oput* process predates colonial rule and frames conflict resolution as a communal and not an individual effort. Because the process emphasizes inclusion and participation, it can be lengthy: victims, perpetrators, witnesses, and community members are encouraged to share their views in a public assembly known as a *kacoke madit* and supervised by a council of elders. The perpetrator is encouraged to acknowledge responsibility or guilt and demonstrate genuine remorse, while victims are encouraged to show mercy and grant forgiveness. Perpetrators may also pay compensation to the victims, which is typically a symbolic gesture that reinforces a perpetrator's genuine remorse. Finally, the process concludes with a *mato oput* reconciliation ceremony, which involves the drinking of a bitter-tasting herb derived from the *oput* tree. The herb symbolizes and transcends the psychological bitterness that prevailed in the minds of the parties during the conflict (Murithi 2002: 292–294).

Some scholars have claimed that the practice of *mato oput* is dehistoricized from its original context and is overromanticized by NGOs, foreign donors, and the Ugandan government. On this theory, *mato oput* (perhaps like *gacaca*) may be an "invention of tradition." One consequence of emphasizing traditional criminal justice is that it reinforces power structures that tend to privilege married men at the expense of women, children, and unmarried men. However, the *mato oput* process appears to retain some connection to Acholi religious beliefs, including that the ceremony is critical to the process of appeasing the spirits of those killed "badly" during the war and preventing future misfortune to the clan. A cleansing ritual may be required for a person to return to villages where massacres took place. Certainly, local justice mechanisms do not preclude a desire for more formal mechanisms of accountability, but they should inform or at least not contradict a formal process. For the Acholi in Northern Uganda, a truth telling process and at least symbolic compensation by perpetrators fulfill genuinely held expectations and desires (Anyeko et al. 2012: 111–112).

An additional constraint on the *mato oput* process is that it may not be representative of all Acholi, and certainly not of Ugandans. Born-again Christians reject such ritual practices as satanic, and the exclusion of women in major decision-making or negotiations reinforces the sexual and gender-based victimization of Acholi women at the hands of the Lord's Resistance Army. Other ethnic groups in Uganda and South Sudan believe that the Acholi are responsible for the conflict, as much of the LRA high command is Acholi. It is not clear that opting for a purely local process would satisfy non-Acholi victims. In addition, the compensation mechanism of the *mato oput* process may deter LRA rebels from returning; traditional justice may be as much an obstacle to peace as the International Criminal Court's indictments (Baines 2007: 107–110). That having been said, embracing the *mato oput* process may be part of a comprehensive restorative justice solution alongside Court prosecutions, at least for lower-level offenders or for returning child soldiers.

A similar grassroots reconciliation process known as *nahe biti* was used in Timor-Leste (East Timor) following the 1999 United Nations-sponsored referendum that eventually led to the country's independence from Indonesia. *Biti* refers to a traditionally-woven mat made out of palm leaves, symbolizing the bringing together of diverse or conflicting views. Like the *mato oput* reconciliation process, the Timorese philosophy of reconciliation is communal and broad-based. While *nahe biti* originally referred to a venue or place where family and wider social issues were discussed, debated, and settled, its meaning has broadened to encompass mending differences, resolving disputes, or settling political conflict after the civil war of 1974. *Nahe biti* was used to reintegrate anti-independence refugees from West Timor in Indonesia, where many offered confessions about their involvement in post-referendum violence in a ceremony typically officiated by a local Catholic priest. The guilty side could have been required to pay a fine or perform community service; in the case of serious crimes, such as murder, the perpetrator was often handed over to the United Nations police for legal inquiries. Due to the traditional set up of the reconciliation ceremony, including traditional dress and the participation of a ritual elder, the process enjoyed local legitimacy (Babo-Soares 2004: 17–27; Hohe 2003: 351).

7.4 Discussion Questions

1. What practical difficulties do you see with customary or traditional criminal justice mechanisms? To what extent should the International Criminal Court respect them?
2. Why do you think the International Criminal Court has focused its case investigations on Africa? Do you think the African criticism of the Court is justified?

7.5 Further Reading

A recent book on Africa's relationship with the International Criminal Court is an in-depth starting point for students interested in this aspect of the Court's membership: *Africa and the International Criminal Court*, edited by Gerhard Werle, Lovell Fernandez, and Moritz Vormbaum (The Hague: TMC

Asser Press 2014). In addition, students may be interested in Kamari Maxine Clarke's complex and wide-ranging book on the International Criminal Court in Africa, particularly for an analysis that engages political and international relations theory: *Fictions of Justice: The International Criminal Court and the Challenge of Legal Pluralism in Sub-Saharan Africa* (Cambridge University Press 2009).

References

Anyeko, K., Baines, E., Komakech, E., Ojok, B., Ogora, L. O., & Victor, L. (2012). "The cooling of hearts": Community truth-telling in Northern Uganda. *Human Rights Review, 13*, 107–124.

Babo-Soares, D. (2004). *Nahe Biti*: The philosophy and process of grassroots reconciliation (and justice) in East Timor. *Asia Pacific Journal of Anthropology, 5*, 15–33.

Baines, E. K. (2007). The haunting of Alice: Local approaches to justice and reconciliation in Northern Uganda. *The International Journal of Transitional Justice, 1*, 91–114.

Bekou, O., & Shah, S. (2006). Realising the potential of the International Criminal Court: The African experience. *Human Rights Law Review, 6*, 499–544.

Blumenthal, D. A. (2002). The politics of justice: Why Israel signed the International Criminal Court statute and what the signature means. *Georgia Journal of International and Comparative Law, 30*, 593–615.

Clarke, K. M. (2009). *Fictions of justice: The International Criminal Court and the challenge of legal pluralism in Sub-Saharan Africa*. New York: Cambridge University Press.

Cole, R. J. V. (2013). Africa's relationship with the International Criminal Court: More political than legal. *Melbourne Journal of International Law, 14*, 1–29.

Gaza flotilla raid: No Israeli charges over *Mavi Mamara*. (2014, Nov 6). *BBC news*. Available at: http://www.bbc.com/news/world-middle-east-29934002.

Hohe, T. (2003). Justice without judiciary in East Timor. *Conflict, Security and Development, 3*, 335–357.

International Criminal Court. (2014, Dec 31). *Declaration accepting the jurisdiction of the International Criminal Court*. Available at: http://www.icc-cpi.int/iccdocs/PIDS/press/Palestine_A_12-3.pdf.

International Justice Resource Center. (2014, July 2). *African Union approves immunity for government officials in amendment to statute*. http://www.ijrcenter.org/2014/07/02/african-union-approves-immunity-for-heads-of-state-in-amendment-to-african-court-of-justice-and-human-rights-statute.

Israel accused of war crimes during campaign in Gaza. (2014a, Nov 5). *The Guardian*. Available at: http://www.theguardian.com/world/2014/nov/05/israel-accused-war-crimes-gaza–amnesty-international.

Jalloh, C. C., Akande, D., & du Plessis, M. (2011). Assessing the African Union concerns about Article 16 of the Rome Statute of the International Criminal Court. *African Journal of Legal Studies, 4*, 5–50.

Levy, A. (1999). Israel rejects its own offspring: The International Criminal Court. *Loyola Los Angeles International and Comparative Law Review, 22*, 207–249.

Martin, M. W., & Bröhmer, J. (2012). The proposed international criminal chamber section of the African Court of Justice and Human Rights: A legal analysis. *South African Yearbook on International Law, 37*, 248–268.

Mendes, E. (2010). *Peace and justice at the International Criminal Court: A court of last resort*. Northampton, MA: Edward Elgar.

Mills, K. (2012). "Bashir is dividing us": Africa and the International Criminal Court. *Human Rights Quarterly, 34*, 404–447.

Murithi, T. (2002). Rebuilding social trust in Northern Uganda. *Peace Review, 14*, 291–295.

Nkhata, M. (2011). Implementation of the Rome statute in Malawi and Zambia: Progress, challenges and prospects. In C. Murungu & J. Biegon (Eds.), *Prosecuting International Crimes in Africa* (pp. 277–304). Pretoria: Pretoria University Law Press.

Palestinian president signs up to join International Criminal Court. (2014b, Dec 31). *The Guardian*. Available at: http://www.theguardian.com/world/2014/dec/31/palestinian-president-international-criminal-court.

Pellet, A. (2010). The Palestinian declaration and the jurisdiction of the International Criminal Court. *Journal of International Criminal Justice, 8*, 981–999.

Reinold, T. (2012). Constitutionalization? Whose constitutionalization? Africa's ambivalent engagement with the International Criminal Court. *International Journal of Constitutional Law, 10*, 1076–1105.

Robinson, D. (2006). Serving the interests of justice: Amnesties, truth commissions, and the International Criminal Court. In J. Harrington, M. Milde, & R. Vernon (Eds.), *Bringing power to justice? The prospects of the International Criminal Court* (pp. 210–243). Ithaca, NY: McGill-Queen's University Press.

Roche, D. (2005). Truth commission amnesties and the International Criminal Court. *British Journal of Criminology, 45*, 565–581.

Sengupta, S. (2014, Dec 8). Palestinians become observers at meeting on International Criminal Court. *New York Times*. Available at: http://www.nytimes.com/2014/12/09/world/middleeast/palestinians-become-observers-at-meeting-on-international-criminal-court.html.

Shaw, M. N. (2011). The Article 12(3) Declaration of the Palestinian Authority, the International Criminal Court and international law. *Journal of International Criminal Justice, 9*, 301–324.

Stewart, D. (2014). *International criminal law in a nutshell*. St. Paul, MN: West Academic Publishing.

Stone, L. (2011). Implementation of the Rome Statute of the International Criminal Court in South Africa. In C. Murungu & J. Biegon (Eds.), *Prosecuting international crimes in Africa* (pp. 305–330). Pretoria: Pretoria University Law Press.

Tait, R. (2015, Jan 7). Palestinians will join the International Criminal Court in April, UN Confirms. *The Telegraph*. Available at: http://www.telegraph.co.uk/news/worldnews/middleeast/palestinian-authority/11331615/Palestinians-will-join-the-International-Criminal-Court-in-April-UN-confirms.html.

Temple-Raston, D. (2005). *Justice on the grass: Three Rwandan journalists, their trial for war crimes, and a nation's quest for redemption*. New York: Free Press.

Zimmerman, A. (2013). Palestine and the International Criminal Court *Quo Vadis*? *Journal of International Criminal Justice, 11*, 303–329.

Index

© Springer International Publishing Switzerland 2015
A. Novak, *The International Criminal Court*, DOI 10.1007/978-3-319-15832-7